Brilliant Activities for

Speaking and Listening for KS2

Ideas to Develop Spoken Language Skills

Years 3–6

John Foster

Brilliant
PUBLICATIONS

We hope you and your pupils enjoy the activities in this book. Brilliant Publications publishes many other books to support, inspire and challenge primary school teachers and pupils. To find out more details on any of our titles please log onto our website: **www.brilliantpublications.co.uk**

Published by Brilliant Publications Limited
Unit 10,
Sparrow Hall Farm,
Edlesborough,
Dunstable,
Bedfordshire,
LU6 2ES

Website: www.brilliantpublications.co.uk
E-mail: info@brilliantpublications.co.uk
Tel: 01525 222292
Fax: 01525 222720

The name 'Brilliant Publications' and the logo are registered trade marks.

Written by John Foster
Illustrated by Jeff Anderson of GCI Illustration Ltd
Cover photograph image supplied under licence by **Fotolia.com**

Printed ISBN: 978-1-78317-231-3
e-pdf ISBN: 978-1-78317-232-0
First published 2017
10 9 8 7 6 5 4 3 2 1

Contents

Years 3–4

Subject		Development Area and Focus	Page
Discussing and debating issues		Literacy / PSHE	
1	What do you think? Pets	To take part in group discussions; listening and responding to different viewpoints.	13–14
2	Discussing an issue: Bullying	To consider the opinions expressed in an article, articulating their own and exploring ideas through role-play.	15–16
3	Points of view: Bad habits	To express ideas, and to consider and evaluate those of others.	17–18
4	Discussing an issue: Junk foods	To discuss various views and give reasons to justify their arguments.	19–20
5	Play safe: A role-play	To engage in role-plays in order to clarify how safe places are to play.	21–22
6	Travelling to school safely	To discuss how people travel to school, offering suggestions for making these journeys safer and giving reasons to support their ideas.	23
Interpreting stories and poems		Literacy / PSHE / Sequencing / Design technology	
7	The golden touch	To understand the narrative structure of a story and its moral. To explore different ways of telling a story.	24–26
8	The figure on the bridge	To discover the sequence of a story through a group discussion, to predict and to speculate how the story might be developed.	27–28
9	The wooden horse	To discuss the main events of a story and its moral and how it might be made into a film.	29–30
10	The old house	To use inference to establish the meaning of a poem, to share their interpretations of it and to produce a performance of the poem.	31–32
11	In the middle of the night	To discuss their responses to a story-poem and to decide how it might be illustrated.	33–34
12	The Fire Monster	To share their responses to a poem and to explore ways of performing it.	35–36
Interpreting facts		PSHE/ Literacy / Science / Design technology/ History	
13	Accidents at home	To interpret a set of facts and figures, to identify the dangers shown in a picture and to draw up a set of safety rules.	37–38
14	Frogs and toads	To study an information text and to decide on the accuracy of a series of statements about it.	39–40

Introduction

This book contains a range of activities designed to develop the spoken language skills of children in Years 3–6. The activities in the first half of the book are designed for use with Years 3 and 4; those in the latter half for use with Years 5 and 6. They meet the requirements of the national curriculum that '*pupils should be taught to develop their competence in spoken language and listening to enhance the effectiveness of their communication across a range of contexts.*' In particular, they develop the children's ability '*to share, respond to and evaluate ideas, arguments and points of view and use evidence or reason to justify opinions.*'

The activities range from interpreting facts and figures and working out the correct order in which instructions and information are given to discussing and debating issues, such as bullying, junk foods and attitudes towards keeping pets. There are also opportunities for role-play, hot-seating and for retelling stories, and for responding to and interpreting poems. The emphasis is on activities in which the children use exploratory talk in order to clarify their viewpoints.

These activities provide the opportunity for teaching children the skills of talking for learning, which need to be taught explicitly. They are designed to help with the direct teaching of the talk skills which will ensure that talk in the classroom fosters learning and to make children aware that the quality of their talk with others matters.

The activities have been selected to develop the skills of speaking and listening across the curriculum, not just in literacy lessons. The chart below shows the subject areas in which exploratory talk is developed.

The science topics include investigating floating and sinking, how shadows are produced and how sound travels. History topics include the Great Fire of London, the Battle of Hastings and the discovery of Tutankhamun's tomb. There are also opportunities for debating PSHE topics, such as bullying and healthy eating, and environmental topics such as pollution and volcanic eruptions.

Years 3–4		
English	PSHE: Debating issues	Links to other subject areas: Investigating topics
Interpreting stories *Activities 7–9*	Social issues *Activities 1–3*	Science *Activities 14, 15, 17*
Interpreting poems *Activities 10–12*	Health issues *Activity 4*	DesignTechnology *Activity 16*
Using persuasive language *Activity 20*	Safety issues *Activities 5, 6, 13*	History *Activities 18, 19, 21*

Years 5–6		
English	PSHE	Links to other subject areas: Investigating topics
Interpreting stories *Activities 30 and 31*	Debating social issues *Activities 22–29*	Science *Activities 36, 37, 38, 41*
Interpreting poems *Activities 32–35*	Health Issues *Activity 40*	Design Technology *Activity 39*
Using persuasive language *Activity 45*		History *Activities 44, 46*
		Geography *Activities 42, 43, 45*

Teacher's Notes

Years 3 and 4

Discussing and debating issues

1. Pets
What do you think? A number of *Talking points* about pets are presented for the children to discuss and to share their own views about pets.

2. Bullying
This activity involves the children studying an article about bullying, discussing the author's views, then sharing their views on the issue.

3. Bad habits
This involves the children in discussing what various people regard as bad habits and expressing their views on what they consider to be bad habits.

4. Junk foods
The children are presented with an article expressing views on the issue of junk foods to read and discuss before sharing their own views.

5. Play safe
A role-play. A group of children discuss whether or not to climb over a fence to explore a building site.

6. Travelling to school
After discussing the dangers that the children at their school face when coming to school and going home, groups are invited to make suggestions as to how travelling to and from school may be made safer.

Interpreting stories and poems

7. The golden touch   After reading the story of King Midas, the children are given a number of *Talking points* to discuss in order to help them to understand the story.

8. The figure on the bridge
This is a sequencing activity. The children are given the opening sentences from a story and have to decide what the correct order is, then to predict how the story might continue. Answer: 12, 4, 9, 1, 7, 5, 14, 2, 15, 3, 8, 6, 10, 13, 11.
A blank storyboard page is needed for this activity.

9. The wooden horse   After reading the story, and discussing its moral, the children are asked to pick out the main events, to draw a storyboard and to share their ideas on how they would make a film of the story.
A blank storyboard page is needed for this activity.

10. The old house   This presents a poem for the children to read and then *Talking points* for them to discuss, comparing their responses and interpretations.

11. In the middle of the night
This consists of a story-poem for the children to discuss and to compare their responses.

12. The Fire Monster   A number of *Talking points* about a poem are presented for the children to discuss.

Interpreting facts

13. Accidents at home   The children are presented with facts and figures to interpret, in this case about accidents at home, before studying a picture which illustrates dangers in the home and drawing up a set of safety rules.

14. Frogs and toads   In this activity, the children are presented with an information text, followed by a series of statements based on the text. They have to decide which of the statements are true and which are false.

15. Floating and sinking   This is a science activity. The children predict whether different objects will float or sink and then are asked to design and make a boat of modelling clay capable of carrying a cargo of 1p pieces.

16. How to draw a hopscotch design
A set of instructions on how to draw a hopscotch design are given and the children have to decide on the correct order for them.

© John Foster and Brilliant Publications Limited

17. Investigating shadows

The children have to carry out a number of experiments making shadows with a torch and to decide what conclusions they can draw from the results.

18. The Great Fire of London

This consists of a quiz to check understanding of the facts about a historical event.

19. The Battle of Hastings

The children are given the facts about the Battle of Hastings and then invited to use them to present news of the battle from the different viewpoints of the Normans and the Anglo-Saxons.

20. Discover the British Motor Museum

This presents an extract from a leaflet for the children to discuss how the information is presented in order to attract people to visit the British Motor Museum.

21. The truth about pirates

Children have to read an article about pirates and pick out what true facts and what myths about pirates it contains.

Years 5 and 6
Discussing and Debating Issues

22. Mobile phones

Children in groups discuss the views expressed in an article 'Why I wish mobile phones hadn't been invented' before considering the benefits of having mobile phones and debating the issue.

23. Are computers a good or bad thing?

This consists of an article about the impact of computers on our lives for the children to discuss before organising a debate on the issue.

24. Sport on TV

In this activity, the children share their views and debate the issue of whether there is too much sport on TV.

25. Space exploration

This involves discussing whether the money spent on exploring space could have been better spent on other things such as eradicating poverty and hunger.

26. Foxhunting

Arguments for and against foxhunting are presented for discussion and the children are then asked to share their views on hunt protests.

27. Zoos

The children are presented with a range of views both for and against zoos for them to discuss.

28. Pollution   The children have to decide which of four pieces of writing best conveys the writer's views on why they are concerned about pollution.

29. The school I'd like   A number of statements from pupils about the school they'd like are presented for groups to discuss before expressing their own views of the school they'd like.

Interpreting stories and poems

30. Robin Hood and the golden arrow
This presents a story about Robin Hood and activities in which the children have to retell the story.

31. How Thor slew the giant
After reading a Norse myth about Thor, the thunder god, the children are given a series of *Talking points* to discuss, before retelling the story in their own words.

32. The Flower   This involves studying a poem and discussing what the poet's message is and how he conveys it.

33. It isn't right to fight   After interpreting the poem, the children debate whether war can ever be justified.

34. There are four chairs round the table
The children are presented with two versions of a poem – a three-verse version and a four-verse version – to discuss and compare.

35. Standing on the sidelines
This involves the study of a poem and discussion of a series of *Talking points*.

Interpreting facts

36. Alligators and crocodiles
After studying an article about alligators and crocodiles, the children are given a number of statements and have to decide which are true and which are false.

37. How sound travels   An explanation is given of how sound travels for the children to discuss. They then have to use the information to make predictions.

38. Predict, observe, explain
This consists of four experiments which show the effect of air pressure. The children are asked to predict what will happen, to observe what happens and to explain why it happens.

39. Planning a shopping centre

The children are given a plan of a new shopping centre and are invited to submit a proposal for the shops and businesses they would put there. They are also invited to share ideas for a new playground.

40. Cycling accident facts

A list of facts about cycling accidents is presented for the children to discuss. They make suggestions for making cycling safer and then plan a video on the dangers of cycling.

41. Sharks

The children have to decide the order in which information should be presented in an article about sharks and to discuss how to avoid being attacked by sharks, before role-playing a scene in which one of the people gives the other tips on how to keep safe from sharks.

42. Southend-on-Sea

The children are invited to compare three pieces of writing about a place and to discuss how they differ according to their purpose and audience.

43. Volcanoes

After reading an article about volcanoes, the children are presented with a number of statements about volcanoes and have to decide which are true and which are false.

44. When I was at school

The children are asked to compare their school with schools in their grandparents' day and to interview an older person about their schooldays.

45. Exploring the Arctic

After studying an article on the dangers of visiting the Arctic, the children are given a list of items they could take with them when going on expeditions to the Arctic and asked to decide which would be the most useful to take.

46. The curse of Tutankhamun's tomb

This is a sequencing activity. The children are presented with an article in which the sentences are in the wrong order. They have to work out the correct order.
The answer is: I, B, G, E, M, A, H, D, J, K, F, L, N, C.

Expressing your opinion in appropriate language

Spoken language underpins the development of reading and writing. It is therefore important that teachers make the children aware of the importance of speech in the classroom. Building up pupils' confidence will encourage their learning in spoken langage and listening skills. It is useful to make them aware of appropriate language to use when expressing their opinions.

Here are some useful phrases you can use:

To give your personal point of view:

In my opinion	I believe that	What I mean is
I'd like to point out that	I understand that	I have heard that
The reason I think this is		

To express a view that is held by other people:

| It is thought that | Some people think | It is generally accepted that |

To agree with an opinion:

| That's a good point | I agree because | I think you are right | That's true |
| I think so too | That's what I said | I can see what you mean | |

To disagree with an opinion:

On the contrary	However	I don't agree because
I don't understand	That's different	That's not what I think
I don't think that's a good reason		

Further games and activities and advice on teaching *Talking Skills* can be found in 'Jumpstart! Talk For Learning' – Lyn Dawes and John Foster (Routledge 2015)

1. What do you think? Pets

In turn, talk about each of the points below and decide whether or not you agree with it and why. Then hold a class discussion in which you share your views.

Talking points

✪ It is not a good idea to give someone a pet as a surprise.

✪ A puppy may be cute but it can grow into a large dog.

✪ A pet can provide company for someone who is lonely.

✪ People who abandon pets should be fined.

✪ Taking a dog for a walk is a good way to get exercise.

✪ There should be a limit to how many pets a person can have in their home.

✪ Looking after a pet teaches you to be responsible.

✪ It can be expensive to keep a pet.

✪ Animals are used to being free rather than kept in a house or in a cage.

✪ Pets should not be trained to do tricks.

✪ Exotic animals should not be kept as pets.

✪ People who ill-treat their pets should be banned from having pets.

✪ It is wrong to keep animals as pets.

In groups

☐ What things does a family need to consider if they want to get a dog?

☐ Make a list including such things as who will be responsible for it, whether it needs a kennel, how much exercise it will need and the cost of keeping it.

☐ Discuss two good reasons why someone in a family might argue for getting a dog and two good reasons why another family member might argue against getting a dog.

☐ Imagine your group has been asked to draw up a canine code on how to keep safe with dogs. Draw up the code then compare it with the Dogs Trust Canine Code which can be found at www.dogstrust.org.uk

Role-play a scene in which two or three members of a family discuss whether or not to get a dog. Hold a class discussion or debate. Put forward the motion that 'People should not keep animals as pets'.

2. Discussing an issue: Bullying

Erica Stewart shares some thoughts about bullying:

Most schools have an anti-bullying policy. Nevertheless bullying continues to be a major problem for children, both in school and outside school, despite the best efforts of teachers and anti-bullying organisations.

The reasons why some people get bullied vary. The victim often stands out for some reason – perhaps their appearance is different or they speak differently. If they don't react when they are bullied, the bullies may leave them alone. But if they let the bully see that they are upset, the bullying is more likely to continue.

So what should you do if you are being bullied? Tell someone, such as a parent, an adult you can trust or a friend. It's worth talking to a friend, even if they can't help you as much as an adult.

Some people suggest it is best to give in and do what the bully wants. But that won't stop the bullying. You shouldn't just put up with it. You should always report bullying.

Some forms of bullying are worse than others. Some people are given nicknames that they do not like. But calling someone by a nickname isn't as bad as calling them names in order to humiliate them. Excluding someone by ignoring them is a form of bullying and mental bullying can be as bad as hurting them physically.

Bullies often say that their victims deserve to be bullied. But no one deserves to be bullied.

The reasons why some people become bullies vary. Often they have been bullied themselves. Bullies are often unhappy. But there's no excuse for making someone else's life a misery. That's a cowardly thing to do.

Here are ten statements about bullies and bullying.

- If you are bullied, you just have to put up with it.
- People who are bullied can make matters worse by the way they react.
- You should always report incidents of bullying.
- It is a good idea to do what the bully wants.
- There is no excuse for bullying someone.
- Mental bullying is as bad as physical bullying.
- If you are bullied, the best person to advise you is a close friend.
- Calling people by a nickname is a form of bullying.
- Teachers turn a blind eye to bullying.
- People who are bullied have only themselves to blame.

In groups

- ❒ Which of these statements reflect Erica Stewart's views?
- ❒ Which of them do not reflect her views?
- ❒ Discuss each of the statements, quoting evidence from the article to support your view.
- ❒ Prepare a list of Dos and Don'ts, giving advice to anyone who is being bullied and present it to the rest of the class.

3.   Points of view: Bad habits

~~~~~~

Ten people tell Erica Stewart the things that they cannot stand.

- The thing that I can't stand is when you are having a meal and someone starts texting. Don't they realise that it's bad manners!

- The thing I can't stand is when people don't close their mouths when they are eating.

- The thing I can't stand is when footballers and other sports stars spit on the ground. It sets a bad example to others. Spitting is unhygienic and spreads germs.

- The thing I can't stand is when people talk loudly on their mobiles, particularly on buses and trains. Why do they have to speak so loudly? I'm not interested in what they have to say. Why can't they keep their voices down?

- The thing I can't stand is people leaving someone in a queue to keep their place. A queue is a queue and when they come back they should have to join it at the back.

- The thing I can't stand is people who take their dog for a walk and don't clear up its mess. It's especially disgusting when they allow the dog to do its business on the pavement.

~~~~~~

- The thing I can't stand is the way some people swear all the time.
- The thing I can't stand is the way some people drop their litter outside fast food restaurants and fish and chip shops.
- The thing I can't stand is when I see people smoking. Don't they realise what smoking does to you?
- The thing I can't stand is people who keep on talking while you are in a cinema. Why can't they just keep quiet and watch the film?

In groups

- Talk about the list of things that the ten people said to Erica Stewart. Rank them in order starting with the thing that annoys the group the most as Number 1.
- What other things do you dislike about the way some people behave? Write down one or two things you can't stand. Then share your views with other members of your group.

Role-play a scene in which a TV reporter interviews a number of people and they tell the reporter what annoys them about the way some people behave.

4. Discussing an issue: Junk foods

It's time to crack down on junk foods

Which would you prefer – another helping of vegetables or a packet of crisps? A bar of chocolate or a piece of fruit? A glass of water or a can of cola?

Eileen Pickersgill says it's time to crackdown on junk foods.

Does what you eat matter? Of course, it does. If you eat the right foods, you will help to keep your body healthy. If you eat the wrong foods, you may become overweight and have a higher risk of developing serious illnesses.

People who eat too many junk foods, such as crisps, chips, biscuits, sweets and chocolate, sugary snacks and soft drinks, are likely to become overweight because these foods contain too much fat, sugar and salt.

So it's time we cracked down on junk food. Yes, we've banned advertising junk foods during TV programmes aimed at children, but top chef Jamie Oliver says that all TV advertising of junk foods before 9pm should be banned.

But it's not enough to crack down on TV advertising, we need to stop the online advertising of junk foods.

We need to put a tax on unhealthy foods that contain lots of sugar and fat.

We need to ban vending machines that sell junk food in places like schools and leisure centres.

We need to stop supermarkets from having sweets and chocolates displayed near the checkouts.

We should show adverts about the dangers of eating too much junk food on TV and in cinemas.

Above all, we need to change our eating habits and eat less junk foods.

In groups

- ❐ Discuss Eileen Pickersgill's views on junk foods.
- ❐ What are junk foods? Why is she so concerned about junk foods?
- ❐ What action does she suggest should be taken to crack down on junk foods?

Discuss the following *Talking points* about junk foods, saying why you agree or disagree with them.

Talking points

- ✪ Adults make too much fuss about junk foods.
- ✪ Junk foods are OK provided you don't eat them too often.
- ✪ People who eat junk foods can't afford to buy more healthy foods.
- ✪ If you have too many soft or fizzy drinks, you are likely to damage your teeth.
- ✪ The risks from eating junk foods are exaggerated.
- ✪ Putting a tax on junk foods is a good idea.
- ✪ Banning adverts isn't going to stop people eating junk foods.
- ✪ People should be able to decide for themselves what they eat.
- ✪ Eating junk foods is addictive. The more you eat them, the more you want them.
- ✪ Junk foods taste nicer than healthy foods.
- ✪ Adverts showing the dangers of junk foods won't stop people from eating junk foods.

On your own

Take it in turns to say whether or not you would sign a petition asking the government to put a 20p per litre tax on soft and fizzy drinks which contain sugar.

5.   Play safe: A role-play

Are you coming or not?

A group of four children are playing near a building site. The builders have finished work and gone home for the night. One of the group suggests that they climb through the fence and explore the site. Another of the group thinks it would be exciting and supports the idea. The third member of the group is unsure whether to go along with the idea, while the fourth argues against the idea.

In groups

❑   Study the illustration.

❑   List all the dangers you can see and talk about why it is dangerous to play on a building site.

❑   Role-play a scene in which the children discuss whether to explore the building site.

❑   How do the two who want to explore it try to persuade the others to go with them?

❑   What does the fourth member say to the others to explain why they are against the idea?

❑ Discuss the different outcomes that could result and replay the scene with different outcomes:

▲ the first two persuade the other two to join them

▲ the fourth member of the group persuades the others not to go in

▲ three of the group go in, but the fourth does not.

❑ Imagine that all four of them go into the site and that one of them has an accident.

▲ What do the others do?

▲ Do they fetch help?

▲ Do they run off and leave the injured person behind?

▲ Do they try to help the injured person to get out of the site before fetching help?

❑ Role-play a scene in which one of the group gets hurt.

❑ In groups of four, imagine that a security guard catches three of the group on the site and lectures the children about the dangers of playing on a building site. The three of them beg the guard not to tell their parents.

6. Travelling to school safely

Imagine that your group has been asked for ideas about how to make getting to and from school safer.

Talking points

First, talk about the dangers faced by people who walk to school, cycle to school, come by bus or taxi, or are driven to school by car.

✪ Are the dangers the same or do they differ for each group?

✪ Is there a particular place where the danger is greatest, such as a corner where people walking have to cross the road?

✪ Do you have to take care when going through the school gates or across the playground because they are used for vehicle access?

✪ Do car drivers sometimes ignore double yellow lines? Do they sometimes double park?

✪ Do you feel safe when coming to school? What could be done to make you feel safer?

In groups

☐ Discuss the safety of where cars park. Would banning them from parking in certain areas make it safer?

☐ Would closing the school gates before school starts and at home time make it safer?

☐ Is there a speed limit outside school? Would introducing a lower limit make it safer?

☐ Would putting up more signs help to make it safer?

☐ What other ideas do you have for making getting to and from school safe?

☐ Make a list of all the suggestions you have made to make travelling to school safer and choose a person from your group to present your ideas to the rest of the class.

7. The golden touch

King Midas had a beautiful daughter with long golden hair called Marigold, whom he loved very much. He was very rich – so rich that one of the rooms in his palace was full of gold. King Midas loved his gold. He loved it as much as he loved his daughter. Although he was very rich, King Midas was greedy. He dreamed of being the richest person in the world.

One night he was woken by a noise in his room. At the foot of his bed stood a boy, dressed in a gold cloak. In his hand, he was holding a golden wand. 'Midas,' he said. 'Is it true that you love gold and want to be the richest man in the world?' King Midas nodded. 'If you had one wish would it be to have as much gold as you wanted?'

'My wish would be that everything I touched would turn to gold,' replied the king.

'In the morning, you shall have your wish,' said the boy. In his hand the golden wand glowed and the boy vanished.

The next day King Midas was eager to see if what the boy said would come true. He was in the palace garden when the sun rose. He reached out to pick a flower and it turned to gold at his touch. He rushed indoors and began to go round the great hall of the palace. He picked up a china dish and it turned to gold. He ran round the room touching things. They all turned to gold, even the curtains and the pictures on the wall.

'I am now the richest man in the world,' he shouted. Just then, his daughter came into the room.

'What's going on?' she asked. When King Midas saw her, he rushed towards her to hug her and tell her the good news. But when he touched her, she turned into a gold statue.

King Midas let go of her and stared. Suddenly, he felt afraid. What had he done? He looked at all the gold around him. What use was it to him? He would give it all away, if only he could get his daughter back.

There was a flash of light and the boy stood before him again. 'Do you still want to be the richest man in the world?' he asked.

King Midas shook his head. 'No!' he cried.

'Then take this wand,' said the boy. He held out a plain wooden wand. 'Touch all the things you turned to gold with this wand and they will become as they were before.'

King Midas took the wand. The first thing he touched was the statue. His daughter stood before him again. Then he went round touching all the other things that he had turned to gold.

And from that day, King Midas set about emptying his room that was full of gold. He used some of it to give to the poor. Some of it he used to build houses, schools and hospitals. He became known for his generosity and his kingdom flourished as his gold touched many lives.

Talking points

- ✪ The boy with the wand taught King Midas a lesson.
- ✪ King Midas was a foolish man.
- ✪ King Midas loved gold more than anything else.
- ✪ The moral of the story is 'Do not be greedy'.
- ✪ King Midas is selfish.
- ✪ A wooden wand is as valuable as a gold one.
- ✪ King Midas was the richest man in the world.
- ✪ There is more than one way to be rich.
- ✪ Rich people must learn to share.
- ✪ King Midas is a clever man.
- ✪ The boy is wiser than King Midas.
- ✪ The message of the story is 'Your family is the most important thing in your life'.

In groups

In your group, discuss different ways of telling the story of King Midas. For example, how would you present it on the radio? How would you make a video of the story? How would you present the story as an item in an assembly? Would you have a narrator? Who would the narrator be? Would you have King Midas telling the story himself? Or would you have one of his courtiers or one of his family?

Produce either a radio version or a video version of the story of King Midas.

8.   The figure on the bridge

The following sentences are from a story by Chris Whitby called 'The figure on the bridge'.

They describe a person making their way through a wood one dark night.

The sentences are in the wrong order.

1   There was a rustling in the bushes.

2   As I came towards the bridge, I glimpsed a figure on the bridge.

3   I stifled a cry.

4   I had to hurry, so I decided to take the short cut through the wood.

5   I caught my foot in a rut on the path and stumbled.

6   A cold shiver went down my spine.

7   I told myself it was only some small animal and nothing to be afraid of.

8   The figure beckoned to me to follow.

9   Although I had been down the path in daylight, I had never been along it in the dark.

10   So it's true, I thought.

11   What should I do?

12   It was a dark night with the moon hidden behind clouds.

13   The old woman had tried to warn me.

14   I wished I had brought my torch with me.

15   It turned towards me.

In groups

❏   Decide on the order in which you think these sentences should go. Then compare your order with that of other groups.

❏   Who do you think the person in the story is?

❏   Where has the person come from?

❏   Where do you think they are going?

❏   Why are they hurrying?

❏   Who is the figure on the bridge?

❏   What is the warning that the old woman gave?

❏   What should the person do?

Talking points

✪   Talk about how the story might continue.

✪   What happens next?

✪   Use the storyboard to plan the rest of the story, then tell your version of the story to the rest of the class.

You will need a blank storyboard page to complete this task.

9.　The wooden horse

The Greeks had been fighting the Trojans for ten years. They had laid siege to the city of Troy, but they had been unable to capture it. Then Odysseus had an idea. They would trick the Trojans into thinking that the Greeks had abandoned the siege.

He ordered his men to build a huge wooden horse with enough room inside for 30 men to hide. He chose 30 of his fiercest fighters. The plan was to leave the wooden horse outside the gates of Troy with his men hidden inside. The rest of the Greeks would pretend to leave, except for one man who was to stay behind in order to convince the Trojans that the Greeks had left and that the wooden horse was a gift.

When the horse was ready, the Greeks towed it up to the city gates. Then they pretended to leave. They burnt their tents, packed up their belongings and boarded their ships. They left the harbour and sailed to a nearby island where they hid and waited.

The Trojans watched as the Greeks left. Then they came out of the city to look at the wooden horse. As they admired it, the man who had been left behind explained that it was a gift from the Greeks to the brave men of Troy who had defended their city so stoutly.

The Trojans were excited that the Greeks had left behind such a wonderful gift. They fetched ropes and tied them to the horse. They were about to drag the horse through the gates when they heard shouting. It was an elderly priest. 'Stop!' he cried. 'Do not trust Greeks who come bearing gifts. We must destroy the horse.'

But no one would listen to him. They opened the gates and dragged the horse inside. Then they started celebrating that the Greeks had gone.

The men inside the horse waited till it grew dark. Then they climbed out, killed the guards and opened the city gates. Under cover of darkness, the Greek ships had returned. The Greek soldiers crept up to the city walls and through the gates. The Trojans realised too late that the wooden horse was a trick. The siege of Troy was over. The Greeks had won.

Talking points

✪ What do you think the moral of the story is?

✪ Discuss the following suggestions and in groups decide which you think the moral is:

    a) never accept a gift from your enemy

    b) don't trust your enemy until you are sure they have given up

    c) people can be fooled if you offer them gifts

    d) it is better to be suspicious rather than to accept things at their face value.

✪ Work with a partner to pick out the main points of the story. Produce a flow chart of the main events. Then compare your flow charts in a group discussion, before taking it in turns to retell the story in your own words.

In groups

❏ How would you make a film of the capture of Troy by the Greeks?

❏ Make a storyboard to show the scenes you would include.

❏ Then make a detailed plan of how you would film one of the scenes. You could produce a script for the scene, allocate roles and make a video of the scene.

You will need a blank storyboard page to complete this task.

The old house stands at the foot of the hill –
Blackened, silent, still.

They say on dark nights
You can hear
The ghost of a laugh
A cry of fear.

That you can see
Beside the wall
A shadowy figure
Gaunt and tall,
Clutching a bundle
Wrapped in a cloak.

That you can see
The swirling smoke
And hear the crackling
Of the fire
And watch as the flames
Leap higher and higher.

The old house stands at the foot of the hill –
Blackened, silent, still.

John Foster

In groups

❐ Read the poem, then discuss the *Talking points* and decide whether or not you agree with them.

Talking points

✪ The old house has been vacant since the fire.

✪ The figure and the fire are not really there.

✪ The bundle is a dead child.

✪ The figure is of a person who escaped the fire.

✪ This is a ghost story.

✪ The fire was started deliberately.

✪ The mysterious figure is a young woman.

✪ People imagine they hear a laugh and a cry.

✪ Some people were trapped and died in the fire.

✪ The poem is meant to frighten the reader.

✪ The poem is about a crime.

Discuss these questions:

1. How do you think the fire may have started?

2. Do you think the fire was an accident or was it started deliberately?

3. Can you find any evidence in the poem to support your view?

4. Do you think the fire occurred recently?

5. Can you point to any evidence to support your view?

How do you feel after reading and discussing the poem?

In your groups plan and perform a reading of the poem. Decide what impression you want your reading to create: Mystery? Suspense? Fear? Pity? Horror?

Experiment with different ways of reading the poem. Think about volume, pace and tone and try different combinations of individual voices and group voices.

11. In the middle of the night

Through the sea-mist
Two small boats glide,
Slipping ashore
On the evening tide.

A man with a lantern
Flashes a light
To warn those on shore,
'We're coming tonight.'

A messenger hurries
From door to door,
Whispering softly,
'They're coming ashore.'

Down the cliff path
Six shadows glide
To the foot of the cliff
Where they crouch and hide.

They watch and wait,
Not saying a word,
Until the sound
Of the oars is heard.

Then, quickly, they hurry
Across the sand.
The barrels are passed
From hand to hand.

They are stacked in the cave
And hidden away
Till it's safe to move them
Another day.

Then, back to their beds
The shadows glide,
While the boats slip away
On the outgoing tide.

John Foster

Talking points

✪ It is a very dark night.

✪ The mist hides the boats.

✪ The men on the cliff path are hard to see.

✪ The boats are ferrying refugees across the sea.

✪ The man with the lantern is sending a warning.

✪ The men on shore are afraid.

✪ The cargo is contraband.

✪ The men on the ship are in a hurry because the tide is turning.

✪ It is too dangerous to carry the barrels up the cliff.

✪ The men hide in a cave till daylight.

✪ The men are pirates hiding treasure.

✪ The men plan to come back to get the barrels later.

✪ The men go home and no one knows they have been out.

✪ The poem tells a story about smuggling.

In groups

❏ Discuss the *Talking points* and say why you agree or disagree with them.

❏ Give your reasons and quote evidence from the poem to support your view.

❏ Do you think 'In the middle of the night' is a good title for the poem? Suggest alternative titles, then compare your suggestions and, as a class, choose another title.

Imagine you are planning to include the poem in a book. How would you illustrate the poem? With one picture or several pictures? Imagine the decision was made to present the poem as a picture strip. Think about what your instructions would be to an illustrator to draw in the eight boxes for the picture strip. Then share your ideas in a class discussion.

12. The Fire Monster

Deep in the boiling belly
Of the volcano
The Fire Monster sleeps:
Wisps of smoke from his nostrils
Squeeze through cracks
In the crater's mouth.

Deep in the boiling belly
Of the volcano
The Fire Monster stirs:
Bubbles of lava from his lips
Foam through crevices
And simmer beneath the surface.

Deep in the boiling belly
Of the volcano
The Fire Monster wakes:
Jets of lava gush from his throat,
Squirting through fissures,
Bursting the crater's dam.

Deep in the boiling belly
Of the volcano
The Fire Monster roars:
Huge chunks of rock spit from his mouth
Red torrents of lava shoot into the sky
To stream down the crater's sides.
In the village in the valley,
The watchers wait
For the Fire Monster's anger to abate.

John Foster

Talking points

✪ The poem provides a picture of a volcano erupting.

✪ The poet imagines that there is a monster inside the earth.

✪ The villagers think the monster is angry.

✪ The villagers think they made the monster angry.

✪ The volcano's crater is compared to a monster's mouth.

✪ The poet describes the monster's body in detail.

✪ The poem is about what happens when a volcano erupts.

✪ The Fire Demon would be a better title.

✪ The verses in the poem all have the same pattern.

✪ There is nothing the villagers can do about the eruption.

✪ The poet uses powerful verbs to describe what happens.

✪ The poet wants you to understand what a spectacular sight a volcanic eruption is.

✪ The poem expresses the strength of a volcanic eruption.

✪ This is a terrifying poem.

In groups

❏ Discuss the *Talking points*, saying why you agree or disagree with them.

❏ How would you illustrate this poem? Draw up the instructions you would give to an artist about how you want them to illustrate the poem.

❏ Prepare a performance of the poem.

© John Foster and Brilliant Publications Limited

13. Accidents at home

Facts and figures

❖ More accidents happen at home than anywhere else.

❖ Children under the age of 5 are more likely to have an accident than older children.

❖ The most common accidents at home are falls.

❖ Each year around 25,000 children under 5 are taken to hospital after being accidently poisoned.

❖ Most accidents happen in the living room or lounge.

❖ On average, around 12 children under 4 suffer a severe injury from a burn or scald each day.

❖ Boys have more accidents than girls.

❖ Many accidents happen in the late afternoon and early evening.

❖ The biggest danger for babies is rolling off a table, bed or sofa.

❖ About 40 children under 5 are taken to hospital each day, because they have choked on something or swallowed something.

❖ Accidents are more likely to happen when an adult is in a hurry.

In groups

❏ Study the *Facts and figures*. Then discuss the following:

- Why do you think falls are the most common type of accident in the home?
- What other types of accident are included in the list?
- Suggest other types of accidents that happen in the home.
- Why do you think boys have more accidents than girls?
- Suggest why children under 5 are more at risk than older children.
- Why do you think most accidents at home happen in the late afternoon or evening?

On your own

▲ Pick out at least one fact which surprises you, then share it with the other members of your group and explain why it surprises you.

▲ Tell the group about any accidents that have happened at home to you or to family members.

▲ What was the cause of the accident? How might it have been avoided?

Study the picture

▲ What dangers can you see in the picture?

▲ What could be done to make the room less dangerous?

▲ Discuss a list of rules that you think everyone needs to follow to make their home a safe place to live.

▲ What rules can you suggest to reduce the risks of a toddler or child:

- being injured in a fall
- being burned
- being scalded
- drinking or swallowing something poisonous
- getting a bad cut
- getting an electric shock

Choose one of the group to report your list of rules to the class.

14. Frogs and toads

Common frog

Features: The common frog has bulging eyes and a hump on its back. Frogs have a smooth moist skin and vary in colour. They are often brown, grey or green. Frogs have webbed feet and strong back legs, so they are able to jump and hop. They are amphibians, which means that they are able to breathe both in the water and on land.

Habitat: Frogs need to live near water and can be found in summer living in long grass in fields and on the edge of woods. In winter, they hibernate when it freezes, burrowing into piles of leaves or in hollows or ditches.

Habits: They are most active at night when they feed on insects, snails and worms, which they catch on their tongues. They like to breed in shallow water where there are algae for the tadpoles to eat, but there are no fish, since fish will eat the tadpoles.

Status: Frogs are not an endangered species, so they are not protected, except that it is against the law to sell them.

Common frog

Common toad

Common toad

Features: Toads have a dry, warty skin and stubby bodies with short back legs, so they crawl and walk rather than hop. Their noses are less pointed than frogs' noses and their eyes stick out less.

Habitat: They are amphibians, but can survive away from water in gardens, woods and fields. They are usually found underneath something, such as a log or stone. They hibernate in winter from October to March.

Habits: Like frogs they are nocturnal creatures and they eat a similar diet to frogs. But they will breed in deeper water than frogs, where fish are present. This is because their tadpoles can produce foul-tasting poisons which protect them from being eaten by the fish.

Status: In spite of the fact that thousands of toads are run over on the roads each year, toads are not classed as an endangered species. They are not protected by law, except that it is illegal to sell them.

In pairs

Read the article on frogs and toads then discuss which of the following statements are true and which are false. Write T or F in the box.

☐	Toads and frogs have similar hind legs.
☐	All frogs are green.
☐	The tadpoles of toads are able to protect themselves more than frogs' tadpoles.
☐	Both frogs and toads are found mainly living underneath such things as logs and stones.
☐	Frogs and toads move about differently.
☐	You can tell the difference between frogs and toads from their skin.
☐	Frogs prefer to breed in more shallow water than toads.
☐	A toad's eyes are different from a frog's.
☐	Frogs are most active during the day, while toads are nocturnal creatures.
☐	Both frogs and toads hibernate in the winter.
☐	It is illegal to catch frogs and toads as they are endangered species.

15. Floating and sinking

Collect these ten different objects: a plastic bottle, a cork, a pencil, a paper clip, a piece of cotton wool, a stone, a rubber ball, a small glass jar, a button, a coin.

In groups, discuss which of the objects you think will sink and which will float. Give reasons for your views and fill in the chart (below).

	Prediction		What happened	
	Float	Sink	Floated	Sank
plastic bottle				
cork				
pencil				
paper clip				
piece of cotton wool				
stone				
rubber ball				
glass jar				
button				
coin				

Design challenge

The challenge is to make a boat of modelling clay capable of holding as many 1p coins as possible. Before you begin discuss what you think will happen if you drop your ball of modelling clay into a bowl of water. Then drop it in the water. What happens? Discuss why you think this happens.

Now mould the modelling clay into different sizes and shapes for your boat. Can you explain why some of the boats you make will hold more coins than others? Whose boat holds the most? Why is theirs the most successful design?

16. How to draw a hopscotch design

Activity: To decide the correct order for a set of instructions.

Hopscotch is a playground game in which a person tries to hop between squares either trying to step on, or avoiding stepping on, a particular square on which a stone or other object has been thrown. Here are a set of instructions for drawing a hopscotch design. The instructions are difficult to follow because they are in the wrong order.

A   Write the numbers one to ten in the squares.

B   Make sure you draw the squares on level ground.

C   A hopscotch design consists of ten squares.

D   Chalk is the best material to use when drawing the squares.

E   The illustration shows a common hopscotch design.

F   Draw a hopscotch design on the ground.

G   The squares need to be big enough for a foot
      to fit in.

H   You can draw other designs, but this is a
      traditional one.

In pairs

In pairs or groups decide the order in which you think these instructions should go. Then compare your group's order with those of other groups.

In pairs

Carry out these experiments creating shadows with a torch and discuss what you learn about shadows.

If you put an object on a table in front of a blank wall and then shine a torch toward the object, you may see a shadow on the wall. Use different objects, such as a glass, a book, a sheet of plastic, a lunch box, a sheet of paper, a piece of cardboard. Can you explain why some objects make a shadow and others do not?

If you put the object in front of a dark curtain instead of a blank wall, what happens? Can you explain why?

If you switch off the torch, what happens to the shadow? What does this tell you about what you need to make a shadow?

If you move the objects closer to the wall, what happens to the shadow?

What happens if you move the torch nearer to the object? Further away from the object?

What do you learn from this about shadows?

How much detail is there in a shadow? Why do you see only an outline of the object? If you shine the torch at the object from different angles, what happens to the shadow?

True or false? (Write T or F in the box.)

☐	A shadow is created by a source of light shining on an object.
☐	The size of a shadow is always the same no matter how far the object is from the surface on which it appears.
☐	The colour of a shadow is always the same.
☐	Some objects do not create a shadow, because the light travels through them.
☐	A clear shadow shows more than just the outline of the object.

In groups

- ☐ Measure your shadow out of doors in sunlight at different times of the day. What do you notice about your shadow?

- ☐ Can you explain the reason for the difference?

- ☐ When you see a bird flying high in the sky, you cannot see its shadow. Yet you can see its shadow when it is flying close to the ground. Can you explain why?

18. The Great Fire of London

❖ The fire started in a bakery in Pudding Lane shortly after midnight on September 2nd.

❖ The fire spread quickly because most of the houses in the city of London were built of wood and many had roofs thatched with straw.

❖ There was a drought in the late summer of 1666 so the wooden houses caught fire easily.

❖ The baker, Thomas Farriner, and his family escaped to the house next door through an upstairs window. Their maid was too frightened to leave and died.

❖ The fire burned for three days and it is estimated that 13,000 homes, housing up to 70,000 people, were destroyed by it.

❖ Attempts to fight the fire were hampered by the narrowness of the streets and the closeness of the houses.

❖ There was panic and chaos as refugees fleeing the fire met firefighters in the narrow alleyways.

❖ People watched the fire from boats on the river Thames.

❖ There were rumours that the fire had been deliberately started by French or Dutch immigrants.

❖ The fire destroyed 87 parish churches and St Paul's Cathedral.

❖ The fire might have been kept to a smaller area if the Mayor of London, Sir Thomas Bloodworth, had acted more quickly to create firebreaks. However, he hesitated because people begged him not to destroy their homes in order to do so.

❖ The temperature at the heart of the fire reached 1700°C.

❖ No one is sure how many people died in the fire. Only six deaths were recorded, but there may have been many more.

❖ The fire was eventually brought under control by using gunpowder to blow up houses to create firebreaks.

In groups

Study the information about the Great Fire. Imagine that one of you is a news presenter, another is a TV reporter at the scene of the Great Fire on Wednesday, September 5th, 1666 and the other members of the group are various people whom the reporter interviews eg the baker, a firefighter, a refugee, the Mayor of London. Act out the report that appears on the TV news.

You have been asked to choose the five most important facts you think people ought to know about the Great Fire of London for a book of Key Facts – British History. List your five key facts. Then compare your list with other people's lists.

Imagine you witnessed the Great Fire of London. Present a report for a radio news bulletin describing it. Make sure you cover the 5Ws – What? Who? Where? When? Why?

On your own, study the facts about the Great Fire of London. Then decide whether the statements below are TRUE or FALSE.

~~~~~~

True or false? (Write T or F in the box.)

☐   The fire started in an inn when a man knocked over a lantern during a brawl.

☐   Everyone in the house where the fire started got out safely.

☐   The fire spread quickly because the houses were made of wood.

☐   The fire was swiftly brought under control thanks to the prompt action of the Lord Mayor.

☐   The fire lasted for three days.

☐   Firefighters managed to save St Paul's Cathedral.

☐   Very few people died in the fire.

☐   The fire spread fast because the houses were only separated by narrow alleyways.

☐   The fire was deliberately started by immigrants.

☐   Firefighters brought the fire under control by blowing up houses to create firebreaks.

~~~~~~

19. The Battle of Hastings

The Battle of Hastings took place on October 14th 1066 between the Anglo-Saxon army led by the Anglo-Saxon King Harold and the Norman army led by William, Duke of Normandy.

Background

Both Harold and William claimed to be the King of England following the death in January 1066 of King Edward, the Confessor, who had no children. Harold had himself crowned King shortly after Edward's death. So William, raised an army and prepared to invade England.

He was able to land in the south of England unopposed on September 28th. This was because the King of Norway had also invaded England claiming he was the rightful King.

King Harold's army had just defeated the Norwegian invaders at the Battle of Stamford Bridge in Yorkshire in which the King of Norway was killed. King Harold was told of William's invasion and hastily marched south to try to stop William advancing into southern England. His army was tired after the battle of Stamford Bridge but Harold was anxious to stop the Normans' advance and they hurried along, covering about 50 miles a day.

The Battle

William's army was estimated to be around 10,000 – about a quarter of the army were cavalry, a quarter were archers and half were infantry. Harold's army was around 7,000. He had a few archers, but most were infantry.

The battle took place on a hill about 7 kilometres from Hastings and lasted from about 9am to dusk. The Norman cavalry charged at the Anglo-Saxons who made a wall of shields. Until mid-afternoon they were unable to break through. Then the Normans pretended to retreat. Some of the Anglo-Saxons thought the Normans were fleeing and charged after them. The Normans turned round and a fierce fight began. The Anglo-Saxons were no match for the Norman cavalry and the Norman archers. Many of them were killed, including King Harold. Legend says he was killed by an arrow in his eye, but he may have been killed by a blow from a sword. With King Harold dead, the Anglo-Saxons fled.

The Norman conquest of England had begun and William was crowned King of England on Christmas Day 1066.

In groups

Imagine that you are reporters from a Norman TV channel, travelling with the Norman army. Discuss the reports that you would have broadcast on the evening before the battle, and the updates you would have given at midday during the battle and at the end of the battle. Then take it in turns to present the reports to the rest of the group.

Repeat the activity, imagining you are reporters from an Anglo-Saxon TV channel. Then hold a class discussion in which you compare how the Norman and Anglo-Saxon reports differed.

'I was there'

Hot-seat one of the class as an Anglo-Saxon soldier who took part in both the battle of Stamford Bridge and the Battle of Hastings and ask them about their experiences.

Then, hot-seat another member of the class as a Norman soldier in William's army.

20. Discover the British Motor Museum

Take a tour around our NEW COLLECTIONS centre to discover 250 cars that you may not have seen before. Go behind the scenes to see our new restoration workshop in action.

Explore...

📢 the world's largest collection of historic British cars in our newly refurbished museum.

📢 take a walk down the Time Road and get up close to cars from past decades.

📢 join a guided tour with one of our enthusiastic guides who will help bring the cars to life.

Experience...

📢 sights, sounds and stories of the British motor industry and get 'under the skin' with our interactive exhibits.

📢 test your knowledge with our activity sheets and trails as you travel through our themed zones. Younger visitors can even cruise in our push along cars.

Enjoy...

📢 a delicious coffee and cake or home-made meal in our cafe. There is everything you need to keep you fuelled throughout your journey.

Or, on sunny days, you can enjoy a picnic, while the kids let off steam in our outdoor play area.

School holidays: During every school holiday themed activities add to the fun with crafts, trails, quizzes and interactive workshops.

Family activities during the year:

SHAUN THE SHEEP ACTIVITIES 24–29 March

MINI MOVERS MONDAYS 18 April then every third Monday of the month

BRITISH MOTOR MUSEUM FAMILY FESTIVAL 31 July

WORLD WAR 1 HISTORY WEEKEND 1–2 October

MUSEUMS AT NIGHT – TORCH LIGHT TOUR 28 October

OUR MECHANICS' CHRISTMAS TRAIL 9 December

CHRISTMAS CRAFTS WEEKEND 10–11 December

In groups

Read the information about the British Motor Museum, then discuss these questions in groups.

What kind of publication do you think this information comes from? A newspaper? A magazine? An advertising leaflet? A poster? A travel guide? Explain why.

Who do you think is the reader that the information is aimed at? Children? Parents? Pensioners? Teachers? Tourists? The general public? People in the motor trade? Give your reasons for your view.

What do you learn about what people can see and do at the motor museum? Make a list of all the things that are mentioned and say which two sound the most interesting.

How does the writer of the information try to make the museum and its attractions appear to be well worth a visit? Point to particular words and phrases the writer uses to try to create this impression.

What does the writer say about the refreshments available at the museum? What do you notice about the words he chooses when writing about the cafe?

Which of the family activity days would you choose to go to if you were offered a free ticket? Which do you think a 6 year old would enjoy most? Which do you think a 16 year old would enjoy? Explain the reasons for your choices.

In pairs role-play a scene in which one person who has visited the museum explains what they saw and did and tells the other person why it is a good place to spend a day out.

Brilliant Activities for Speaking and Listening for KS2

21. The truth about pirates

Louis Peacey reveals the facts and the fictions about pirates.

Ask someone to draw you a picture of a pirate and the chances are you'll get a picture of a scruffy man with a beard, an eyepatch on one eye, a skull and cross bones hat on his head, a scarf round his neck and a parrot on his shoulder. He may also have a pistol and a cutlass in his belt, and a wooden leg and be drinking rum on the deck of a galleon, peering at a treasure map.

How accurate is such a picture? Not very, I'm afraid. It's based more on books, such as Robert Louis Stevenson's 'Treasure Island' and Disney films rather than on what the pirates were actually like.

Few, if any, had a skull and crossbones hat. They were often scruffy and didn't shave, so they had beards, but only those with an injured eye wore an eyepatch. They wore scarves called bandannas and some of them kept parrots to sell when they reached land. However, the parrots weren't likely to say 'Shiver me timbers.' That phrase was first used in 'Treasure Island'. It's true that pirates and other sailors had their own slang, but it was different from the language used by pirates in books and films.

Some pirates had wooden legs and there may have been one or two with hooks, where a hand had been cut off. In fact, pirates who had their legs amputated often caught an infection and died.

Most pirates didn't bury their treasure. Most of them sold any gold and jewels that they found, then spent the money drinking and gambling. Only very occasionally did they bury it. And they didn't make maps to show where the buried treasure was. The majority of pirates were ordinary sailors who couldn't read or write.

Pirate ships were usually small one-masted ships rather than galleons with three masts. It's true that some of them flew skull and crossbones flags.

Life on board a pirate ship was hard. Food was often scarce and they were as interested in what food and water was on board any ship they could capture as in what treasure it was carrying.

Real pirates weren't swashbuckling heroes like the ones in Pirates of the Carribean. And, there's no evidence that they made prisoners walk the plank. That's another thing about pirates that comes from books and films.

In pairs

Pick out five facts about pirates that you learn from the article and five myths. Then share your lists with another pair.

Say whether you agree or disagree with these statements:

* Pirates drew maps showing where they buried treasure.
* A typical pirate had a skull and crossbones tattoo.
* Pirates' ships usually had only one mast.
* A pirate's life was glamorous.
* Few pirates wore eyepatches.
* Many pirates had a wooden leg.
* Pirates did not make prisoners walk the plank.
* Pirates of the Caribbean gives an accurate picture of what a pirate's life was like.
* Pirates sold the gold and jewels they stole and spent the money drinking and gambling.
* Very few pirates buried the treasure they took.

Choose one of the group to be hot-seated as a pirate. The other members of the group ask questions about 'life as a pirate'.

Prepare a radio programme 'The truth about pirates' in which you include interviews with a pirate and a historian who talk about the myths about pirates.

22. Mobile phones

Derek Stuart explains why he wishes mobile phones hadn't been invented!

Mobile phones are a nuisance and a danger. I seriously wish they had never been invented. You can't go anywhere without having to listen to someone blathering on about where they are and what they are doing. If I had my way, I'd ban the use of mobile phones on trains and other forms of public transport.

I'd ban them in restaurants too. You go out for a meal with your family and friends and your conversation is constantly being interrupted by irritating ringtones and people talking loudly on their mobiles. I also find it infuriating when people reply to text messages while at the dining table.

Even more infuriating is going to the cinema or theatre and someone's mobile starts ringing.

People say that mobiles enable people to feel safer. They enable parents to know where their children are.

You can no longer walk down the street without the risk of someone barging into you because they are talking on their mobile and not looking where they are going. Mobile phones are dangerous too. You see people driving while talking or texting. It's as dangerous as drink-driving.

But are they really safe? No one knows for sure what the long term effects of using mobiles are. They may seriously damage your health. We lived happily enough without them. I wish mobiles had never been invented.

In groups

- ❑ Discuss each of the reasons Derek Stuart gives for saying why he wishes mobile phones had never been invented. Explain why you agree or disagree with his views.
- ❑ Discuss what you consider to be the benefits of having mobile phones. What would life be like without mobile phones?

23. Are computers a good or a bad thing?

Ian Ashendon asks: 'Do the benefits of computers outweigh the drawbacks?'

Computers have changed the world. The Internet has made communication easier and faster. We can now connect with people across the globe instantly. We can chat with our friends on social networking sites or hold business meetings by Skype.

Computers have revolutionised the way we obtain information. All kinds of information is there for us at our fingertips. Whether we want to find out what is on at the local cinemas or to research a topic for our homework , it is all accessible on our PC.

Computers also provide us with entertainment. We can download films, watch videos on YouTube and play computers games. Computers can give us hours of fun. But all this comes at a price. Parents find it hard to control their children's use of the Internet. Children can access unsuitable sites and make friends with strangers, who pose as young people.

Also, there's the problem of cyber-bullying. Bullies can anonymously post hurtful remarks on social networking sites about other children.

Computer games can be addictive. Young people can spend all their free time on the computer instead of being outdoors playing.

It's true that you can look up anything on the computer, but you have no way of knowing if the information you're being given is correct.

Then there's the problem of terrorists using the Internet to plot attacks. Also, extremists can use the Internet to recruit people and brainwash them.

The technological revolution has brought many benefits, but it has brought problems too.

In groups

❑ Discuss each of the points Ian Ashendon makes in his article and rank them on a 5-star scale (1 being not very important and 5 being very important). Compare how your group ranked the points with how other other groups ranked them. Then, on your own, decide whether you think overall computers have been a good or bad thing and take part in a debate on the issue.

24. Sport on TV

Is there too much sport on TV? Many families are divided on this question. Some parents say there's too much football, but many men and boys disagree.

Some people say that children are becoming couch potatoes because they spend so much time watching sports on TV. Others argue that watching sports encourages young people to take up sports.

Some sports like football get plenty of coverage on TV, but minority sports are neglected. Women's sports are far less likely to be shown on TV. There's too much of some sports, but not enough of others.

And why should you have to pay to watch major sports events? Surely events like Wimbledon, the Ashes and the Grand National should be free on TV for everyone to watch.

Major sporting events attract millions of viewers. But people who aren't interested have plenty of other channels to watch or they can just switch off, instead of moaning. The same applies to people who moan about regular programmes being moved to make way for live broadcasts.

Sport on TV encourages gambling and there's a risk of more people becoming addicts. Also, TV companies paying huge sums of money to show sports programmes has had the effect of making footballers and other sports stars greedy. Footballers are now paid ridiculous amounts each week and transfer fees are absurd.

Are people right to complain that there is too much sport on television? Or should we look forward to the day when tiddlywinks, croquet and conkers are shown on TV?

In groups

- ❒ Discuss what arguments the writer puts for the view that there is too much sport on TV and the arguments against such a view.
- ❒ Do you think the writer was a man or a woman? Give your reasons.
- ❒ Does the article give a balanced view of the arguments? What do you think the writer's own view is? Give your reasons.

- Role-play a scene in which a journalist interviews:

  a) a television executive who argues that TV is right to show so much sport

  b) a member of a campaign group CASOT – Campaign Against Sport On TV.

- Hold either a debate or a whole-class discussion in which you share your views about whether there is too much sport on TV.

25. Space exploration

Is exploring space a waste of money?

The space race

The space race! The space race!

What has it all been for?

Stockpiling satellites

To wage a nuclear war?

The space race! The space race!

Wouldn't it have been more worth

Spending all that money

To improve life on Earth?

Derek Stuart

Exploring space could help mankind by solving the problem of overpopulation and we could even discover new life forms.

Of course, we should explore space. Who knows what we will find? We'll never know, if we don't try to find out.

The exploration of space has produced many benefits, such as the development of new materials, personal computers and solar energy.

Expensive missions to the moon and beyond are madness when we have unsolved problems here on earth like hunger and diseases.

Money that is currently being spent on space exploration could be spent trying to find solutions to problems, such as climate change and drought.

Role-play

Choose three people to role-play a TV studio discussion in which an interviewer asks the other two people to say why they hold different opinions on the value of space exploration. One of them thinks it is invaluable, the other thinks it is a waste of money.

26. Debating an issue: Foxhunting

What people who go foxhunting say ...

'It's exciting. It's lots of fun galloping after the hounds once they get the fox's scent.'

'Hunting's been going on for hundreds of years. It's a fine old tradition.'

'Foxhunters care about the countryside. They are conservationists.'

'Foxes are pests and hunting them controls their numbers.'

'Hunting is a humane way of controlling the fox population.'

What people who are against foxhunting say ...

'Animals have rights. It's cruel to chase after helpless animals.'

'Foxes which are hunted die painful deaths.'

'Foxes aren't pests. They kill rabbits which eat farmers' crops.'

'If people want to have the excitement of riding across the countryside, they can go drag hunting.'

'About three times as many foxes are killed on the road each year as are killed by hunting with hounds. Foxhunting isn't an effective way of controlling the fox population.'

In groups

Discuss the arguments people use for and against foxhunting. Decide what your opinion is and why. Then prepare a speech expressing your view. You can organise a debate on the motion: This house believes that there should be a total ban on foxhunting.

What pro- and anti-foxhunters say about hunt protests ...

'Anti-hunt protests are OK so long as people protest peacefully.'

'Hunt protesters go too far, breaking kennels and releasing dogs, laying false trails and threatening people.'

Would you ever consider taking part in a protest against foxhunting? Give your reasons.

Some people are prepared to break the law in defence of animal rights. What is your opinion of their actions?

Is it right to keep animals in zoos?

Here are some different opinions about keeping animals in zoos.

'Zoos are important in saving animals from extinction. Animals that are in danger of becoming extinct in the wild can be bred in captivity then released back into the wild.' **Conservationist**

'Zoos are cruel. Animals often get ill, because of the poor conditions they live in.' **Vet**

'Keeping animals in captivity doesn't teach you anything about what animals are like in the wild. It only shows how an animal behaves when it is behind bars.' **Animal psychologist**

'Zoos give scientists the chance to study animal behaviour.' **Zoo keeper**

'We should be protecting animals in their natural habitats. Then we wouldn't need to put them in zoos to protect them.' **Campaigner**

'Zoos give people lots of pleasure and the chance to see animals they wouldn't otherwise see.' **Zoo owner**

'We have no right to take animals out of their natural habitats and stick them in a cage in a country that they don't belong in.' **Animal rights activist**

'On the whole, animals in zoos are kept in comfortable conditions and are well fed.' **Zoo worker**

'You don't need zoos to teach you about animals. You can learn all about them from documentaries and videos.' **Student**

'Zoos teach you about the need for conservation. They make you aware what man's behaviour is doing to animals and make you realise why we need to protect them.' **Game warden**

'Zoos are educational. You can see animals being fed and listen to talks about them and their habits.' **Teacher**

'The idea of breeding animals in zoos sounds good. But it's hard to get some animals to breed in captivity. Also, animals bred in zoos aren't always able to survive when released into the wild.' **Researcher**

In groups

Discuss the arguments for and against keeping animals in zoos. Then hold a class debate in which you share your views before taking a vote on the view that all zoos should be closed down.

28. Debating an issue: Pollution

Read the four pieces of writing which were entered for a competition in which children were asked to write about 'Why I'm concerned about pollution.'

It's a big problem

There are several different types of pollution. Some pollution is caused by cars, some by people burning coal on their fires and then there is industrial pollution.

There's air pollution like the smog in China. Some cities have banned cars from entering the city on certain days to cut down on the pollution caused by exhaust fumes. I think that's a good idea.

We need to stop producing so much rubbish too. Pollution is a big problem.

Jason

Act now before it's too late

Pollution is a problem that concerns us all. The chemicals we release into the air from burning fossil fuels affect the ozone layer which leads to global warming. They affect the air we breathe, causing chest infections, such as bronchitis and asthma.

Chemical waste produced by factories is emptied into rivers and lakes, killing fish and other wildlife. Or it is released into the air causing acid rain, which erodes buildings and destroys forests.

Then there is pollution of the sea. It is estimated that by 2050 there will be more plastic in the sea than fishes. And, of course, there's the nuclear waste that has been dumped in the sea.

We need to act now do something about pollution before it is too late.
Samir

Stop throwing things away

I don't understand those people who sound off about pollution, then go around dropping litter everywhere. We could save lots of precious resources by sorting out our rubbish when it is collected. Lots of councils do this anyway.

We rely on cars which cause pollution and we waste lots of things which could be recycled. If we're going to save the planet for future generations, then we all need to reuse things rather than throw them away.
Penny

A major challenge

Pollution is one of the major challenges that the world faces. It causes climate change, which is producing a rise in temperature, melting the ice caps and leading to a rise in sea level. If we don't do something about it, there will be more flooding in the future.

It means we need to change how we live now. We must stop depending on fossil fuels and find cleaner, greener ways of producing energy.
Nasreen

In groups

Imagine you are the judges of the competition and decide which of these pieces you think should be chosen as one of the winners.

THE SCHOOL I'D LIKE

All the teachers would treat everybody the same instead of having favourites.

In my ideal school, you wouldn't have to wear uniform. You could wear what you like.

You would be able to choose what to do.

There would be no exams.

There would be no homework!

There would be a games lesson every day.

You would be able to wear make-up and jewellery.

You would only go to school in the morning.

You would be allowed to choose whether to stay in or go out at breaktimes.

Anyone who disrupts a lesson would be sent home.

There would be no bullying.

You would be able to have chips and burgers for lunch every day.

You wouldn't have to do games, if you didn't want to.

We wouldn't have to listen to boring assemblies.

Everyone would have the opportunity to learn a musical instrument.

The school rules would be drawn up by the pupils.

In groups

☐ Discuss each of these views of what the children say they would like to have in their ideal school.

☐ Pick out the statements you agree with.

☐ Are there any other things that you would like to have in your ideal school?

☐ Choose someone from your group to share your ideas with the rest of the class.

MY IDEAL SCHOOL: WHERE KIDS RULE!

Long ago there was a man called Robin Hood, who was an outlaw. He lived in a forest near Nottingham called Sherwood Forest with several other outlaws. They were always laughing and joking, so they were known as Robin Hood and his merry men.

Robin Hood and his merry men would stop anyone riding through the forest and demand money from them. Then they would share the money with the poor people who lived in the villages near the forest.

The poor people said Robin Hood was a hero. But the rich people were angry. They said that Robin Hood was a thief. He must be captured and put in prison.

They went to Nottingham castle and complained to the sheriff. The sheriff did not want to risk sending his men into the forest to arrest Robin Hood, so he made a plan. He would hold an archery contest. The prize would be a golden arrow. Robin Hood had boasted that he was the best archer in the whole of Nottingham. The sheriff knew that Robin Hood would be unable to resist the challenge of entering the contest.

He knew also that he would be able to recognise Robin Hood, because the merry men always wore green. When Robin Hood took his turn in the contest, the soldiers would arrest him.

Robin Hood was determined to enter the contest. But he knew that he must trick the sheriff. So he called a meeting of the merry men and told them what they must do.

On the day of the contest, there was a huge crowd. The sheriff was on the lookout for men dressed in green. He spotted a man in a green tunic and immediately had him arrested. But it turned out he was the shoemaker's son. So the sheriff ordered him to be set free.

Men dressed in all colours took part in the contest. When it was the turn of a man wearing blue, the crowd all jeered. He had a huge bow that looked too big for him. But when he drew back the bow and took aim, his arrows flew straight. Six times he shot and six times his arrows hit the centre of the target.

The crowd cheered and the man in blue was presented with the golden arrow. The sheriff was so impressed that he sent a message inviting the man in blue to become one of his soldiers. But the man had disappeared into the crowd.

Once he was back in the forest, Robin Hood took off the blue clothes which he had been wearing and the merry men took off all the different coloured clothes they had worn. Robin laughed as he showed them the golden arrow.

Next day, Robin Hood got one of his men to write a message to the sheriff. He said that now everyone knew that Robin Hood was the best archer in the whole of Nottingham. Robin signed the letter. Then, he wrapped the message around the shaft of the golden arrow. That night, as darkness fell, Robin Hood made his way to the castle. Then he fitted the golden arrow into his bow and shot it over the castle wall.

A servant found the arrow and took it to the sheriff. When the sheriff read the message, he flew into a rage. His plan had failed. Robin Hood had tricked him. He tore the message into pieces and threw them into the fire.

~~~~~~

From outside the castle came the sound of laughter. The poor people of Nottingham laughed as news spread of how Robin Hood had tricked the sheriff.

On your own

Retell the story in your own words. (You might find it helpful to prepare a number of cards with key words on them to remind you what is essential to include in your retelling.)

In groups

❒ Take it in turns to retell the story either to other people in your group or to the rest of the class.

❒ Choose one of the class to be hot-seated as Robin Hood and/or the Sheriff of Nottingham giving a press conference after the archery contest. In pairs, prepare the questions you are going to ask them.

❒ Imagine you were asked to make a film of the story. In your group, produce a storyboard, showing the scenes that you would include. Produce a script for your film and then make a video of the story.

❒ Adapt the story for radio. How would you tell the story? Would you have a narrator? What scenes would you include? Produce a script. Then make a recording of your adaptation.

❒ Compare your film adaptation with your radio adaptation. Which do you think worked better? Why?

31. Interpreting stories: How Thor slew the giant

The Vikings believed in many gods. They thought that the gods behaved like superhumans and lived in a great city called Asgard.

The chief of the gods was Odin, the father of all the other gods. Odin was said to have only one eye, because he had traded the other eye for a drink from the well of wisdom. He knew everything that was going on, because he had two ravens that could speak. They flew above the world and told him what they saw.

Odin was guarded by two fierce wolves and rode a horse with eight legs, which could travel through the air faster than the wind. One day, Odin was out riding and he came to the land of the giants, where he met the giant called Hrungnir. 'That's a fine horse you have there,' said the giant.

'He certainly is,' said Odin. 'He can run faster than any other horse. That horse there wouldn't stand a chance against him.' He pointed at the giant's horse called Golden Mane, which was standing nearby. So confident was Odin that his horse could outrun any other horse that he said, 'I bet my head that he can run faster than your horse.'

The giant was furious. Who was this stranger that boasted he had a faster horse than Golden Mane?

'I'll bet he can't,' he said and with that he mounted his horse and off they charged.

They raced across fields and through forests, over hills and mountains, across snow-covered plains and through streams and rivers. Odin's horse led the way and, no matter how hard the giant tried, Golden Mane could not overtake him.

They raced on until they passed through the gates of the city of Asgard and the giant found himself in the city of the gods.

The gods invited him to have a drink with them. The giant was angry that he had lost the bet and became drunk. He threatened to kill all the gods, except for two goddesses who he would take captive. One of the goddesses was the wife of Thor, the strongest of Odin's

Brilliant Activities for Speaking and Listening for KS2
70

© John Foster and Brilliant Publications Limited
This page may be photocopied for use by the purchasing institution only.

children, who had a mighty hammer which he used to create storms, thunder and lightning.

When Thor was told what the giant said, he lifted his hammer and prepared to strike the giant dead. The drunken giant accused Thor of being about to attack an unarmed man and challenged Thor to a duel. Thor agreed and the giant went off to arm himself.

The duel was held in a field near the land of the giants. The giant walked onto the field wearing stone armour, carrying a stone shield and a wielding a huge whetstone above his head. He planned to hurl the stone at Thor.

All of a sudden, there was a flash of lightning, a crash of thunder and Thor appeared on the field. He wore iron gloves and brandished his deadly hammer. Giving a mighty roar, Thor hurled his hammer at the giant, who threw the stone at Thor. The hammer struck the giant's head and he was killed instantly.

But the stone shattered into a thousand pieces against Thor's head. One piece of the stone buried itself in Thor's forehead and remained there for the rest of his life.

In groups

Discuss each of the following *Talking points* about the story and say whether or not you agree with them.

Talking points

* This is a story about revenge.
* The story shows that the gods were all powerful.
* The moral of this story is: be careful not to annoy the gods.
* The giant is responsible for his own death.
* The giant did not stand a chance against Thor.
* Odin tricked the giant by leading him into the city of the gods.
* The gods deliberately got the giant drunk.
* The giant was jealous of the gods.
* Thor killed the giant to save the other gods.
* The giant underestimated Thor's power.

Take it in turns to retell the story in your own words to the rest of your group, then discuss which retelling was the most successful and why.

'This room,' said the teacher,

'was called a conservatory.

In it you will see "The Flower".

Can you remember what a flower is?'

'Please, sir, it's a kind of plant.'

'Well done, Rose.

It's a kind of plant.

How is it different from the plants that we grow today?'

'Please, sir, you can't eat it.'

'Well done, Violet.

You can't eat it.

And where was it grown?'

'Please, sir, in a garden.'

'That's right, Primrose.

In a garden.

And what was a garden?'

'Please, sir, a piece of land beside a house.'

'That's right, Iris.

A piece of land that people who lived in a house would claim that was theirs.

And what did they do in the garden?'

'Please, sir, they grew flowers.'

'Well done, Daisy.

They grew flowers. And why did they grow flowers?'

'Please sir, to look at.'

'That's right, Poppy'

'Please, sir, and to smell.'

'Well done, Hyacinth.

They grew flowers to look at and smell.

But we don't grow flowers today.

Why not?'

'Please, sir, because they are banned.'

'That's right, Marigold.

And why are they banned?'

'Please, sir, because they serve no useful purpose.'

'Exactly. Well done, Lily.

So look at The Flower.

As you will see

It serves no useful purpose.

It is there only to remind us

why we no longer grow them.'

'Oh, but it's pretty,' said Primrose.

'And its petals are soft,' said Poppy.

'And it smells so nice,' said Hyacinth.

'It's beautiful,' said Rose.

'Do not be deceived,' said the teacher.

'It serves no useful purpose.'

John Foster

In groups

❏ Discuss the following *Talking points* about the poem, saying whether you agree with them, giving reasons for your views.

❏ Prepare a reading of the poem. Talk about the tone of voice you are going to use for the teacher/guide and for the children. Discuss which group gave the most effective reading and why you thought it was the most effective.

❏ Talk about how you felt after reading and discussing the poem. Then write a paragraph about the poem in which you express your views about the poem and its message.

Talking points

✱ The man in the poem is teaching the children how valuable flowers are.

✱ The children have never seen a flower before.

✱ The poet has the same attitude towards flowers as the man in the poem.

✱ The children understand why flowers have been banned.

✱ The poem is a warning.

✱ The children are amazed when they see The Flower.

✱ The poem tells us why we shouldn't grow flowers.

✱ The children are being brainwashed.

✱ There is a good reason why all the children have names that are the names of flowers.

✱ The man in the poem convinces the children that flowers are unimportant.

You said, 'It isn't right to fight.'

But when we watched the news tonight,

You shook your fist and said

You wished the tyrant and his cronies dead.

When I asked why,

If it's not right to fight,

You gave a sigh.

You shook your head

And sadly said,

'Sometimes a cause is just

And, if there is no other way,

Perhaps, you must.'

John Foster

In groups

☐ Who are the two people in the poem?

☐ Suggest what they see as they watch the television news.

☐ Why does one of them shake their head?

☐ What is that person's attitude to tyrants? Do you share their view?

☐ What question is asked in the poem?

☐ Why does the person sigh before answering?

☐ What answer is given? Do you agree or disagree with their answer?

☐ The poem raises more questions about fighting than it answers. Discuss this view: the poet is a pacifist and this is an anti-war poem. Do you agree?

In pairs, prepare a reading of the poem to present to the rest of the class.

Hold a debate on the issue of whether war can ever be justified.

Version one

There are four chairs round the table

There are four chairs round the table,
Where we sit down for our tea.
But now we only set places
For Mum, for Terry and me.

We don't chatter any more
About what we did in the day.
Terry and I eat quickly,
Then we both go out to play.

Mum doesn't smile like she used to.
Often, she just sits and sighs.
Sometimes, I know from the smudges,
That while we are out she cries.

John Foster

Version two

There are four chairs round the table

There are four chairs round the table,
Where we sit down for our tea.
But now we only set places
For Mum, for Terry and me.

We don't chatter any more
About what we did in the day.
Terry and I eat quickly,
Then we both go out to play.

Mum doesn't smile like she used to.
Often, she just sits and sighs.
Sometimes, I know from the smudges,
That while we are out she cries.

Why did he have to leave us?
Why did he have to go?
Was it something that I did?
I suppose I'll never know.

John Foster

Read the two versions of 'There are four chairs round the table', then discuss the *Talking points* and say whether or not you agree with them and why.

Talking points

✪ The children go out to play because they find their mother's crying upsetting.

✪ The mother cries because she misses her husband.

✪ The man in the poem has left his wife.

✪ The mother is a widow.

✪ Both versions are sad.

✪ The first version is a poem about the mother's feelings.

✪ In the second version the focus is on the child.

✪ They are two different poems rather than two versions of the same poem.

✪ In the fourth verse, the child blames himself for the father's absence.

✪ The fourth verse shows that the child doesn't want to know why the father has gone.

✪ Both versions of the poem are about loss and how we deal with it.

In groups

❑ Discuss which version of the poem you prefer and why. Imagine you are the editors of a book of poems. Which version would you choose to put in the book? Why?

❑ How would you illustrate the two versions of the poem? Would the illustration be the same for both versions? What brief would you give to the illustrator as to how to illustrate the poem(s)?

35. Standing on the sidelines

I'm standing on the sidelines,
Kicking a ball against a wall,
Developing my skills,
Waiting for your call.

I'm standing on the sidelines,
Waving at each train,
Wondering if, and when or where
I'll catch a ride again.

I'm standing in the courtroom,
Accused of the crime
Of trying to scrape a living
While idly killing time.

I'm standing in the corridor.
I'm waiting in the queue.
I'd rather not be here.
But it's what I have to do.

John Foster

In groups, discuss the following *Talking points* about the poem.

Talking points

- ✪ This poem is about people who are outsiders.
- ✪ This is a poem about being excluded.
- ✪ The poem is about someone who is unlucky.
- ✪ This poem is about people who are looking for a job.
- ✪ The person in the queue is unhappy.
- ✪ The person is waiting for a phone call.
- ✪ This is a sad poem.
- ✪ The poet is trying to make a point about the way society treats people.
- ✪ The person in the poem feels rejected.
- ✪ The person in the poem is not guilty of any crime.
- ✪ This is a poem about being unemployed.
- ✪ The person in the poem is trapped in a situation they would like to have avoided.
- ✪ The person in the poem is angry.
- ✪ The poet sympathises with the person in the poem.
- ✪ This is a poem with a powerful message.
- ✪ The most effective verse is the third verse.
- ✪ The four verses are about the same person.
- ✪ The poet is angry about the way some people are treated.
- ✪ This is a pessimistic poem.
- ✪ Do you think 'Standing on the sidelines' is a good title? Discuss the view that it is misleading and suggest an alternative title.

Alligators and crocodiles are both reptiles. Two of the main features of reptiles are that they are cold-blooded and have a dry scaly skin. They can swim and survive in water, but they are not amphibians, because they lay their eggs on land. Amphibians lay their eggs in water and have gills, so that they can breathe in water, but they can also live on land.

Alligators and crocodiles have eyes and nostrils on top of their heads, so they can lie in the water with most of their bodies hidden as they wait for prey. They can also stay underwater for up to a quarter of an hour.

They often lie in the sun to get warm because they are cold-blooded. You may see pictures of them with their mouths open. This is called 'gaping' and they do this so as not to get too hot.

Alligators are only found in America and in China, but crocodiles are found in many countries around the world, including Australia. Both crocodiles and alligators have scales. They also have long tails, sharp teeth and short legs, with webbed toes. But they are different colours. Alligators are darker, while crocodiles have scales that are a greyish-green.

Another difference is in the shape of the snout, which is more rounded in alligators. The lower and upper jaws of alligators are the same size. You can tell if it is a crocodile rather than an alligator because the fourth tooth of a crocodile sticks out when its mouth is closed.

Alligators and crocodiles are found in swamps. Alligators are mainly found in fresh water. Crocodiles are found in both fresh water and salt water.

Both alligators and crocodiles are carnivores and will attack humans, but crocodiles tend to be more aggressive. Neither crocodiles nor alligators make good pets!

~~~~~~~~~~~~~~~~~~~~~~~~~~~~~~

In groups

Discuss the statements below and decide if they are true or false. Write T or F in the box.

☐ Both crocodiles and alligators are found in Australia.

☐ Crocodiles and alligators can stay underwater for 10–15 minutes.

☐ Crocodiles and alligators are amphibians.

☐ Alligator scales are different from crocodile scales.

☐ Alligators live mainly in salt water.

☐ Crocodiles and alligators lie with their mouths open so that they can quickly snap up any prey that passes.

☐ Crocodiles and alligators are carnivores.

☐ Crocodiles have upper jaws and lower jaws that are the same size.

☐ Alligators are more aggressive than crocodiles.

☐ Crocodiles have long legs and short tails.

☐ Crocodiles are cold-blooded but alligators are warm-blooded.

Crocodile

Alligator

~~~~~~~~~~~~~~~~~~~~~~~~~~~~~~

A sound is made because something moves. A guitar produces a note when it is plucked. A machine makes a noise when it is working. Human beings and animals produce noises by making their mouths and throats move.

Some sounds are natural sounds. Others are artificial sounds; they are caused by or are by-products of things human beings have made.

A sound is made by a movement backwards and forwards, called a vibration. It's like when you throw a stone into water: it makes small waves or ripples. The waves spread outwards from the point where the stone enters the water. Sound also travels in waves. They spread outwards in all directions from the object making the sound.

Sound waves can travel only when there is a substance to carry the vibrations. They can travel faster through some solid and liquid things than through air. It depends on how easily the substance vibrates.

Sounds can travel a long way. The North American Indians used to put their ears to the ground, to listen for the sound of their enemies. They could hear horses' hoof beats from several kilometres away.

✦ Discuss how sound travels in waves.
✦ Talk about which sounds are natural and which are artificial. Make a list of at least five examples of each type.
✦ Discuss why North American Indians sometimes put their ears to the ground.
✦ Sounds travel through some materials and substances more easily than others. How well do you think sound will travel through wood, plastic, cardboard, glass, metal, leather? How could you find out if your prediction is correct?
✦ Tap on the top of a table with a pencil and listen. Then put your ear against the table and tap on it again. Which sound is louder? Can you explain why?
✦ Tie two or three spoons to the end of a piece of string about a metre long. Swing the spoons gently so they strike each other. Listen to the sound they make. Then tie the string round a finger and put the finger in your ear. Swing the string so that the spoons knock together.

Listen to the sound. How is it different? Can you explain why?

✦ Do you think sound can travel through space? Give your reasons.

✦ In a thunderstorm, do you hear the thunder before you see the lightning? Can you suggest why this is?

✦ What is an echo? What do you think causes an echo?

✦ Suggest how echoes can be used by ships to find out the depth of water in a lake or sea.

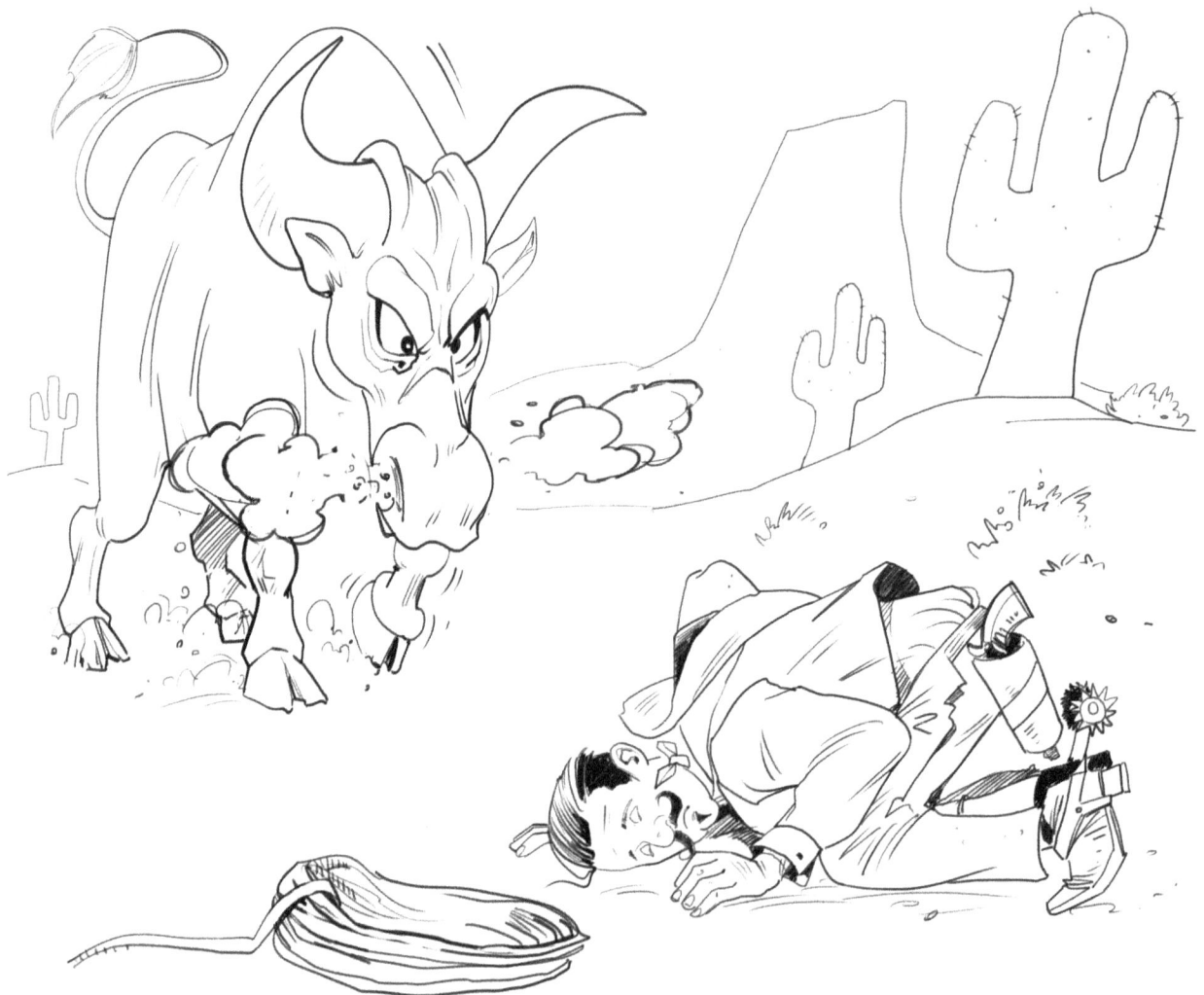

38. Predict, observe, explain

1. Read the instructions for each of these experiments and predict what you think will happen in each case.

2. Carry out each of the experiments and talk about what actually happened.

3. Can you explain the reason for what happened in each case.

Experiment 1

✦ Put a glass under a tap and fill it right to the top with water.

✦ Slide a thick piece of card over the top of the glass.

✦ Hold the card firmly in place and carefully turn the glass upside down.

✦ Take your hand away from the card.

What happens? Why?

Experiment 2

✦ Place a thin piece of wood about the length of an old wooden ruler (30cms) so that one end is sticking out over the edge of a table.

✦ Spread a large sheet of newspaper over the end of the wood which is lying on the table. Flatten it out as much as you can with your hand.

✦ Give the end of the wood that is sticking out a sharp knock downwards.

What happens? Why?

Experiment 3

✦ Use some strong thread to hang two apples from the ceiling. Put them about 2 cms apart.

✦ Blow on the apples to try to move them apart.

What happens? Why?

Experiment 4

✦ Take a thin piece of card about the size of a playing card and stick a pin through the centre of the card.

✦ Put an empty cotton reel over the card, so that the pin goes through the hole in the centre of the cotton reel.

✦ Hold the card flat on your hand, then bend down and blow through the cotton reel.

✦ Then take your hand away and continue blowing.

What happens? Why?

A new shopping centre

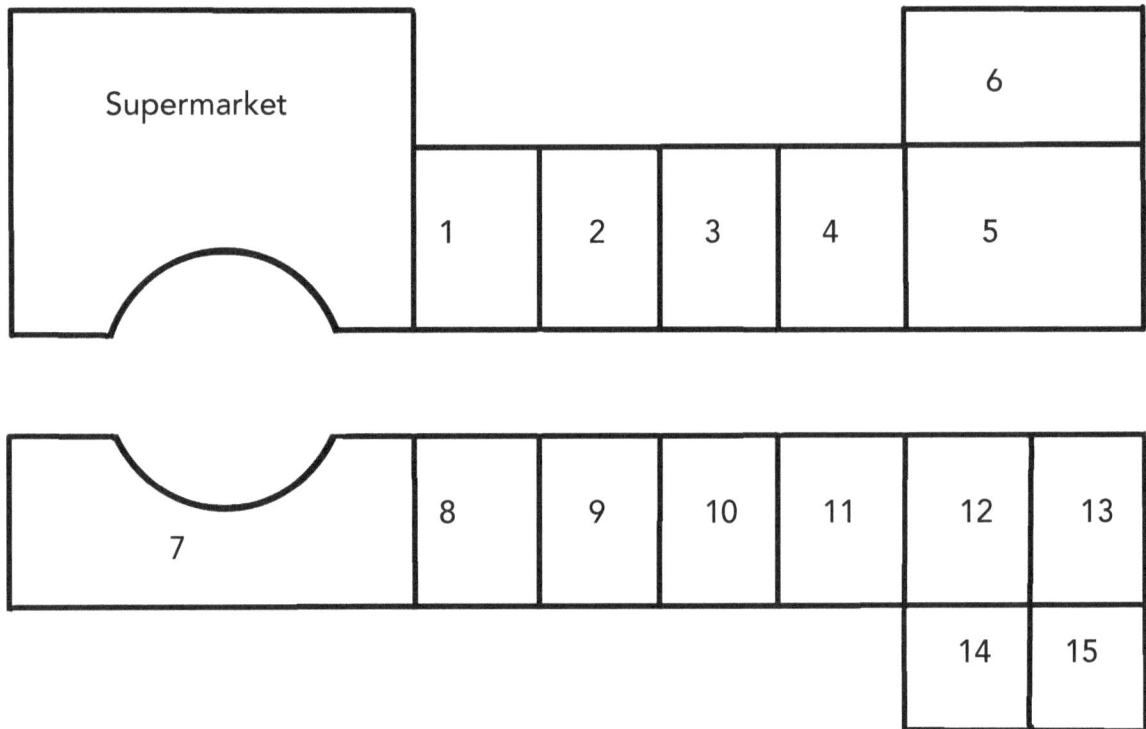

In groups

☐ Study the plan above of a new shopping centre. There are 16 spaces for shops and businesses. It has already been decided to use the largest space for a supermarket. Decide what shops and businesses you would put in the other 15 spaces. Talk about how a shopping centre often contains businesses such as banks and estate agencies, offering services, as well as shops selling different goods and maybe a cafe, pub or restaurant.

☐ Share your plans with those of other groups, and decide whose plan is the best and why.

A new playground

Plan a new playground. Imagine the local council has given your group a grant of £100,000 to turn a piece of wasteland into a playground. Discuss how you would spend the money, explaining what equipment you would buy and prepare a PowerPoint presentation of your ideas.

40. Cycling accident facts

* Cycling casualties have increased in recent years.

* 10–15 year olds are more at risk than any other age group.

* Males are more likely to be involved in cycling accidents than females.

* Most cycling accidents occur in urban areas.

* About 80% of cycling accidents happen in daylight.

* The majority of cycling accidents occur between 3pm and 6pm and between 8am and 9am.

* There are more cycling accidents between May and September than between October and April.

* Accidents involving children are often caused by doing tricks or riding too fast.

* More adults are injured in cycling accidents than children.

* Three-quarters of cycling accidents occur at or near a road junction.

* Particular dangers for cyclists are turning right and negotiating roundabouts.

* Riding off the pavement onto the road is a significant cause of a number of cycling accidents.

Source ROSPA

In groups

☐ Read the following suggestions for making cycling safer and, in turn, discuss the facts and what you think are the reasons for them.

* Children should not be allowed to cycle on the road until they are 9 years old.

* Cyclists who do not wear helmets should be taken to court and fined.

* It should be compulsory to wear reflective clothing when cycling.

* Cyclists should not be allowed on main roads which do not have cycle lanes.

* Cyclists should have to take lessons and pass a cycling test before being allowed on the road.

* Cyclists should have insurance for their bicycles, just as car drivers have for their cars.

* There should be more cycle lanes.

* If you ride a bike that is more than five years old you should have to have it tested to make sure it is safe.

© John Foster and Brilliant Publications Limited

This page may be photocopied for use by the purchasing institution only.

Brilliant Activities for Speaking and Listening for KS2

87

❏ Discuss these suggestions. Which do you think is the best one? What other measures can you suggest to make cycling safer?

❏ Imagine your group has been asked to produce a short 2 minute video aimed at making children aware of the dangers of cycling. Make a detailed plan of the video to present to the rest of the class.

41. Sharks

The sentences below are from an article about sharks, but they are in the wrong order. In small groups decide on their correct order. Then compare your order with the order decided by the other groups.

A.   Instead, they have skeletons made of cartilage, which is lighter and more flexible than bone.

B.   All sharks are carnivores.

C.   Unlike most animals, sharks can move both their upper and lower jaws,

D.   They are predators at the top of the food chain.

E.   The first sharks appeared millions of years ago.

F.   Sharks have several rows of teeth, so they can replace the teeth which they lose.

G.   Sharks are a type of fish but, unlike fish, they do not have bones.

H.   But there are less than 100 shark attacks each year and about 10 deaths from shark attacks.

I.   Sharks have as many as 2000 teeth.

J.   The teeth are arranged in rows and when they lose or damage a tooth, another replaces it.

K.   Sharks are becoming an endangered species.

L.   Sharks have a very strong sense of smell, which can detect blood in the water from miles away.

M.   Teeth of the Great White Shark are used to make necklaces and other jewellery.

N.   People are far more likely to die in a road accident than be killed by a shark.

O.   Whenever there is a shark attack, it is reported in the news.

P.   They are caught for their meat and to make shark fin soup.

Top tips:

How to avoid being attacked by a shark:

❖ Don't wear shiny jewellery or bright patterned clothing.

❖ Don't swim alone. Always swim in a group.

❖ Avoid splashing about.

❖ Don't go too far from the shore.

❖ Avoid areas where there are fishermen.

❖ Keep away from areas near waste pipes discharging sewage.

❖ Don't swim near estuaries where the water is muddy.

❖ Don't go swimming where there are seals.

❖ If you are bleeding, don't go swimming.

❖ Keep away from sandbars and places where the ocean floor slopes steeply.

❖ Don't let pets go swimming with you in case they start splashing.

❖ If you see a shark, don't play dead.

❖ Don't ignore warning notices.

❖ Avoid swimming at night, at dawn and at dusk.

❖ Wear a device on your ankle which sends out an electronic signal to keep sharks away.

In pairs

Discuss the reasons for each piece of advice. Then role-play a scene in which a TV interviewer asks a marine biologist what measures a person should take to avoid being attacked by a shark.

© John Foster and Brilliant Publications Limited

42. Understanding the author's intention: Southend-on-Sea

About Southend 1

Southend is a seaside resort town in Essex. It is situated on the north side of the Thames estuary. There is a regular train service into central London, 40 miles away to the west. It is famous for its pier, which is the world's longest pleasure pier, being over a mile and a quarter long. Southend was a very popular holiday destination until the 1960s when overseas holidays became more affordable. It still attracts over six million tourists a year.

About Southend 2

Southend offers more than all the traditional pleasures of a seaside holiday. We offer a range of great attractions for the whole family to enjoy, including the longest pleasure pier in the world, Adventure Island fun park and Sea-Life Adventure Aquarium. History buffs can step back in time at some fascinating places such as Southchurch Hall and Prittlewell Priory and take a ride on the shortest cliff lift in the UK. Our town centre offers a unique shopping experience and with over 300 mouth-watering places to eat and a dazzling live music and nightlife scene, the visitor is really spoilt for choice.

About Southend 3

Enjoy free days out in Southend building sandcastles with the kids and unwind with all the pleasures of a seaside holiday on our award-winning beaches. Ride the railway to the end of the longest pleasure pier in the world, get involved in hands-on fun at a museum or run free among the many parks and gardens. Ride the waves for exhilaration or admire the skills of expert windsurfers and kitesurfers. Dare to try thrilling rides at Adventure Island, one of the UK's favourite fun parks. Then, relax over a meal, before taking in an evening show at the theatre or cinema or enjoying an evening stroll along the sea front.

In groups

☐ Imagine your family are thinking of going on holiday to Southend. On your own pick out what you think are the five most important things you learn about Southend from the three descriptions. Then share the list with the rest of the group.

☐ Which of the three descriptions tells you the most about Southend as a holiday resort and which gives you the least information about it as a holiday resort? Why do you think this is?

☐ What sort of publication do you think each of the descriptions come from: a pamphlet, a leaflet, an advertisement, a guide book, a reference book, an information website? Give your reasons.

☐ What kind of audience do you think each of the writers is aiming at – children, teenagers, parents, single people, older people, a general audience? Give reasons for your view.

☐ Compare the style of the three descriptions. Talk about how the first description is more impersonal than the second and third descriptions, how the second writer uses personal pronouns to describe what Southend offers and how the third writer addresses the reader directly by using the imperative verb form.

☐ Discuss the words and phrases that ...

  a) the second writer

  b) the third writer

  ... use to make Southend appear attractive as a holiday resort.

  Do you think you and your family would enjoy a holiday at Southend? Give your reasons.

☐ Produce a PowerPoint presentation in which you try to make your town appear attractive as a holiday destination. Present the information in the style used by either the second or the third writer.

43. Volcanoes

Volcano

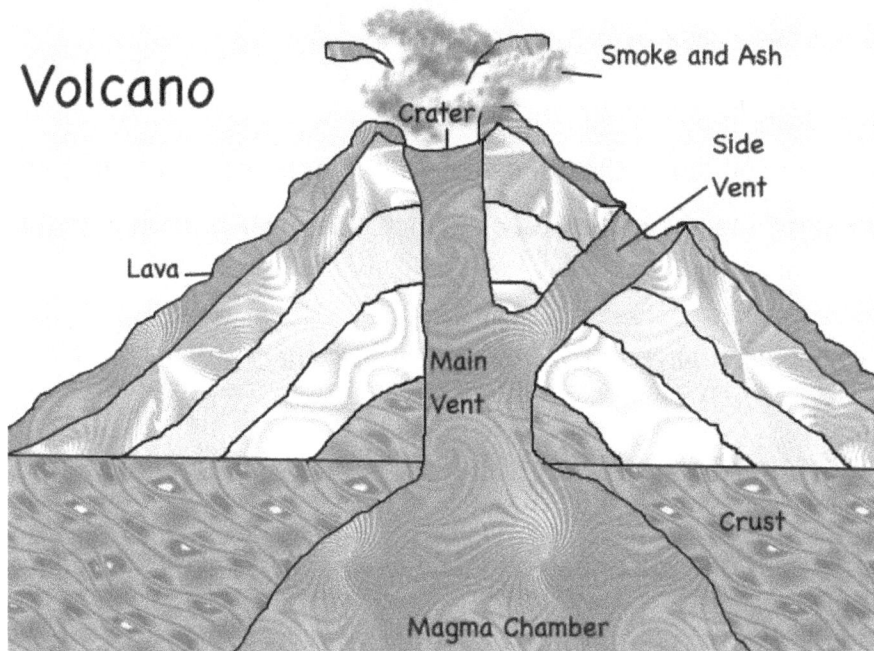

In the centre of the earth it is very hot, so hot that the rock has melted. This molten rock is called magma. In some places, the magma from near the surface breaks through an opening in the earth's crust. Clouds of gas, magma and ash are hurled into the air. The opening through which the material escapes is called a volcano.

When a volcano erupts, it looks as if a mountain is on fire. Ash can be thrown up to 30 kilometres above the surface and clouds of ash may block out the sun. Often a crater is formed and the molten rock becomes lava which flows down the sides of the crater crushing everything in its path. A stream of lava can travel at up to 50 mph. Lava may continue to pour out of a volcano for several days and there may be several eruptions over a period of weeks.

When the volcano erupted on the Caribbean island of Martinique in 1902, the whole population of the island, over 30,000, was killed except for two people. One was a shoemaker. The other was a prisoner. The stone walls of the prison saved his life. The explosion when a large eruption occurs releases more energy than hundreds of nuclear bombs. The loudest sound produced in modern times was made when the volcano erupted on Krakatoa in 1883.

Volcanoes are found in many parts of the world, particularly around the Pacific Ocean,

© John Foster and Brilliant Publications Limited

~~~~~~

but there are none in Australia. Volcanoes are found under the sea and they may erupt and cause an island to be formed. A volcanic eruption led to the appearance of a new island called Surtsey Island off the coast of Iceland in November 1963. Volcanic eruptions under the sea can be the cause of a tsunami.

Some volcanoes are likely to erupt at any time. These are called active volcanoes. Others which have not erupted for some time are said to be dormant, while volcanoes that have not erupted in modern times are said to be extinct. But scientists are unable to predict exactly when an eruption will occur.

The Earth is the only planet with active volcanoes, but there are extinct volcanoes on Mars.

In groups
Read these statements about volcanoes and decide whether they are True or False and write T or F in the box.

☐	Volcanoes are found all over the world.
☐	A volcano may erupt at any time.
☐	Scientists can predict when a volcano is going to erupt.
☐	Volcanoes are found on Mars as well as on the Earth.
☐	Volcanic eruptions often last for several days or even weeks.
☐	Volcanoes can erupt under the sea.
☐	A volcanic eruption can trigger a tsunami.
☐	Volcanoes can throw ash up to 30 kilometres above the earth.
☐	A volcanic eruption produces enormous amounts of energy.
☐	Volcanoes are active on other planets in our solar system.
☐	An extinct volcano has had no eruptions for a very long time.
☐	During an eruption, lava races down the side of a volcano very fast.
☐	Over the centuries, many people have been killed by volcanoes erupting.

~~~~~~

Schools were very different when I was young. They used to ring a bell which echoed round the village and you had to be lined up ready to go into the classroom by the time it stopped.

In the classroom the teacher stood on a wooden platform called a dais. We sat in rows at wooden desks with lids. We kept our books in our desks. There was a hole in the corner of the desk in which there was a china pot to put ink in. We didn't have plastic biros. We used wooden pens with metal nibs. You dipped your nib into the ink and then wrote with it. If you put too much ink on the nib, it would drip onto the paper and make blots. We had special paper called blotting paper which we used to soak up the ink.

Every day we practised our handwriting. We had to copy a verse from the Bible which our teacher wrote on the blackboard with a piece of chalk.

We practised our reading too. The teacher wrote words on the blackboard and we had to read them together. We all had the same reading book and we took turns to read from it.

We did sums every day and had to learn to do long division as well as to add and subtract. There were no calculators to help us. We copied sums from the board, chanted the times tables and we had to work out problems like how many tomatoes we would be able to buy for a shilling if six tomatoes cost two pence.

The teacher kept a strap on her desk. Children who were naughty got their hands strapped.

At playtime we had a drink of milk. The milk was in small glass bottles and you drank it through a paper straw.

In the playground, we played marbles and hopscotch. We also played tag and the girls practised skipping. In autumn, we played conkers.

We had PE lessons in the playground. We wore plimsolls and our vests and shorts. We did stretching exercises and running on the spot.

On some days we did country dancing. There was a gramophone in the hall. The teacher played records and we danced.

Stanley Lewis

In pairs

✦ Discuss how the school Stanley Lewis describes is different from your school.

✦ Is there anything in your school that is still the same?

✦ If you had gone to that school, what would you have liked and disliked about it?

✦ Interview an old person to find out what their school days were like. Prepare a series of questions to ask in the interview, then take it in turns to report to the class what you found out about their school days.

45. Exploring the Arctic

A visit to the Arctic can be dangerous. Derek Stuart offers some advice.

◆ Beware polar bears. They may look cuddly and cute in the zoo, but they are dangerous predators who will attack you if you're not careful.

◆ Look out for mosquitoes and other insects which flourish in the short Arctic summer. Make sure you have plenty of repellent.

◆ Watch out for white-outs. A blizzard can blow up quickly, obliterating everything, so you can become disorientated. Stay indoors if a storm is forecast.

◆ Don't get dehydrated. You probably won't feel the need for water when it's cold. But drink plenty of it or you'll get dehydrated.

◆ Slap on the suncream. The sun reflects off the ice and snow at all angles and it's easy to get sunburn.

◆ Watch out for windburn. The wind can reach 60mph or more. You can get burnt through windburn, too.

◆ Cover your skin. Wear plenty of warm clothes to protect yourself from frostbite.

◆ Don't get trapped out of doors. Your body will quickly cool down and there's the danger of suffering from hypothermia, which occurs when your body temperature falls too low.

◆ Tread carefully where you go. Wear a good pair of boots and watch out for icy patches in the snow and be especially careful when walking across snow-covered ice. There may be cracks in the ice which you can't see because of the snow.

In pairs

Take it in turns to summarise Derek Stuart's advice. Then see how much of his advice you can convey in just 50 words.

In groups

Imagine you are going on an expedition to the North Pole. You have to decide what items you will need to take with you to ensure that you keep safe and warm. Make a list of everything you would need. Then compare your lists in a class discussion.

A survival kit

Study the list (below) of items you might pack in a survival kit and choose those you would take on a trip to the Arctic. Then discuss which items you would take to the jungle. If you were limited to ten items, which ten would you take?

- A Swiss army knife
- A mobile phone
- Bandages
- A compass
- A ball of string
- A life jacket
- A radio
- Binoculars
- Money (US dollars)
- Antiseptic cream
- A full water bottle
- An axe

- A torch and spare batteries
- A mobile phone charger
- Malaria tablets
- Paper and pen
- A hammer and nails
- A mosquito net
- A box of matches
- Suntan cream
- Insect repellent
- A packet of painkillers
- A packet of firelighters

46. The curse of Tutankhamun's tomb

The sentences (below) describe the events which followed the discovery of the tomb of the young Egyptian pharaoh Tutankhamun. Some people think these events resulted from a curse put on the men who entered the tomb. The sentences are in the wrong order. In groups discuss what the correct order of the sentences should be.

A   Then came the sudden death a few months later of Lord Carnavon who had financed Carter's search for the tomb.

B   It brought him instant fame, but at a huge price.

C   Whether or not such an inscription existed is unclear.

D   Lord Carnavon appears to have died from an insect bite on his left cheek.

E   The first evidence of the curse was the death of Carter's pet canary, which died on the day he first entered the tomb.

F   Maybe there is a rational explanation for these events.

G   For Carter and those who entered the tomb were haunted by what became known as the curse of Tutankhamun's tomb.

H   He died in Cairo and, at the moment of his death, the lights all went out throughout the city.

I   In 1922, Howard Carter discovered the tomb of the young pharaoh Tutankhamun.

J   When Tutankhamun's mummy was unwrapped, it was found that he had a mark on his left cheek exactly where Lord Carnavon had been bitten.

K   Several other people who were connected with the excavation of the tomb also died in mysterious circumstances, including the person who X-rayed Tutankhamun's mummy.

L   But some people claim that the curse of Tutankhamun's tomb was responsible.

M   His servant told him it was attacked by a cobra.

N   Above the entrance to the tomb there was said to be these words 'Death will come to those who disturb the tomb of a pharaoh.'

Assessing your skills: What makes a good talk?

When you have to give a talk to your classmates, it can be a daunting task. So what can you do to make it go well? Jackie Abingdon offers some advice.

How to give a good talk

Have an interesting beginning that grabs the audience's attention.

Make sure you make eye contact with the audience.

Try to include some humour in your talk. But beware! Telling jokes is dangerous. They can fall flat.

Don't just read your talk: Make some cue cards.

Stand up straight. Don't slouch.

Use gestures.

Vary the tone of your voice to add emphasis.

Don't speak too fast.

Make sure that there is a clear ending.

Don't mumble. Talk clearly.

Speak up, so that you can be heard at the back of the room.

Look and sound confident, even though you may be feeling nervous.

Try to involve the audience by asking rhetorical questions.

Use this sheet to talk about what makes a good talk. On your own, pick out what you consider to be the five most important pieces of advice that Jackie Abingdon offers. Then share your views.

Take it in turns to present a talk to the class. Use the sheet to assess the talks people make. First, comment on all the things a person did well, then point out two or three things for them to work on, in order to improve their performance the next time they have to give a talk.

Assessing your skills : Participating in group discussions

Use this sheet to assess how well you contribute to group discussions.

	My assessment	Peer assessment	Teacher assessment
I listen attentively to what other people have to say.			
I wait until there is an opportunity for me to speak.			
I keep to the subject that is being discussed.			
I give reasons for my views.			
I quote evidence to support my arguments.			
I do not interrupt when other people are talking.			
I refer back to what people have said previously.			
I respect other people's opinions.			
I can take on different roles in the group.			
I help to refocus the discussion if it goes off task.			
I speak clearly and do not mumble or shout.			
My targets for improvement are			

Assessing your skills: Debating issues and presenting arguments

Jason Feister offers advice on how to present an argument in order to try to persuade people to agree with your point of view, for example when taking part in a debate.

Get off to a good start

It's important that you grab the audience's attention right from the start. So it's a good idea to begin with a strong statement, such as 'It's about time we faced up to the fact that we must take more care of the environment.'

Another good way of beginning is to start with a question: 'How much longer are we going to go on harming the environment?'

State your reasons clearly

Make sure you express the reasons for your viewpoint clearly as separate points. Give evidence to support your arguments.

Include evidence to support your point of view. Quote facts and statistics, such as, 'Drowning is the third highest accidental cause of death of children in the UK each year.'

State the reasons why you disagree with the opposite point of view.

Say what the opposite point of view is and state clearly the reasons you don't agree with it.

Include questions

Including questions can have a dramatic effect, particularly if they do not require an answer. 'Isn't it obvious that it's dangerous to fly your kite where there are pylons?'

Involve the audience:

Addressing the audience directly can help to get them to agree with you. For example, 'How would you like to be locked in a cage all day?'

End emphatically:

Don't let your talk just come to a halt. End it on a high note. 'That's why we must be prepared to stand up for our beliefs, whatever the cost.'

Assessing listening skills

Individually, read these statements and make a list of those that you think apply to you. Then discuss your views in a group, before setting a target of how you are going to try to improve your listening skills.

1. I always let people finish before I give my point of view.
2. I am prepared to change my mind if I find an argument convincing.
3. I always pay attention to what another person says in a discussion.
4. I often summarise what another person says to make sure I have understood them.
5. If I think the person speaking is wrong, I lose interest and stop paying attention.
6. I pick up on points other speakers make and refer back to them.
7. I listen carefully, because I think you can learn a lot from listening.
8. I find it hard to listen. My mind keeps wandering.
9. I always ask for clarification, if I find an argument hard to follow.
10. I am an active, rather than a passive, listener.
11. I know talking helps you to learn, so I always listen attentively.
12. Listening to other people has helped me to understand what I think.

Assessing the development of reasoning skills

Use this sheet to assess the development of your reasoning skills.

On a scale of 1 to 5 rank how good you think your reasoning skills are :

    1: Excellent

    2: Very good

    3: Good

    4: Not very good

    5: Poor

Then show your assessment to your teacher and discuss what you can do to improve them.

- [ ] I can express my point of view, giving reasons in statements such as 'I think ... ', 'I know ... ', 'In my opinion ... '.

- [ ] I can quote evidence to support reasons.

- [ ] I can present arguments against someone else's point of view and explain why I reject them.

- [ ] I can make decisions based on reasons.

- [ ] I am prepared to change my mind if given a convincing reason for doing so.

- [ ] I am not influenced by emotional statements unless they are based on sound reasoning.

- [ ] I can evaluate evidence.

- [ ] I can debate an issue, referring to the arguments presented by other speakers.

- [ ] I can develop an argument logically, step-by-step.

- [ ] I can see the flaws in an argument and give reasons why the argument is flawed.

www.ingramcontent.com/pod-product-compliance
Lightning Source LLC
Chambersburg PA
CBHW080841270326
41927CB00013B/3065